HAVING FAITH
to Live
by FAITH

By Misty Lee Hicks

ACKNOWLEDGEMENTS

I owe a *big* thank you to my mom, Eva Carter Hicks, for spending countless hours with me pouring over this book, correcting grammar and empowering me to be a better writer. Mom, thanks for your unconditional love and for knowing how to bring out the best in me.

There is no person on this earth that I admire more than you!

Thanks to my sister, Stormy Massey. We laughed and cried as we talked about the influence Helen had on our lives. We retold Helen's stories until they found their way to these pages. Thanks, womb mate, for being my biggest cheerleader and for holding my hand in this journey through life.

IN MEMORY OF HELEN WRIGHT

M s. Helen, I trust that you are looking down at me from heaven and smiling. Perhaps elbowing Jesus in the ribs, pointing your finger at me and giggling just a little. The words on the pages of this book pale in comparison to the wonderful life you lived. I cannot do your life justice but, alas, I tried.

Thank you for your patience and for your transparency. I was captivated by your relationship with Jesus and, eventually, I fell in love with Him too. Thank you for lovingly and generously sharing everything with me!

I am growing older now and it will not be long before we see each other again. I am looking forward to getting a big hug from you as you stand on your tippy toes and throw your arms around my neck. What a wonderful homecoming that will be!

TABLE OF CONTENTS

INTRODUCTION

My friend Helen Wright is a strong role model. Her life is filled with stories of God's love and faithfulness. She trusted Christ to meet her every need and He did. Helen's simple faith and miraculous life made a lasting impression on me.

Helen helped me answer questions such as: Where does faith come from? How can I have more faith? Can I pray so I will see miracles happen in my life? These pages contain the wisdom needed to live a life of faith. This book covers basic things such as Bible study, how to hear God's voice, how to experience His presence, and how to see ourselves as He sees us. The book also covers deeper things such as exploring the covenant God made with us, learning how to live in grace instead of law, and understanding God's sovereignty, to name a few.

Each truth is illustrated by a story that will enable the reader to have a better understanding of the Word of God. This book is filled with Helen's stories, along with stories from others who have impacted my life, and with personal stories from my own experiences working in ministry and as a missionary in Africa. These stories are motivating.

I pray this book will propel you into an intimate relationship with Jesus and into a life of faith.

Chapter One

VEGETABLE SOUP, A RED COAT AND BALLET SLIPPERS

A lot can happen in a moment; some moments change our lives forever.

I had never met anyone like Helen. Although she was a petite lady, she was larger than life. She lived what she believed. The amazing things that happened to her over and over again made her life extraordinary.

We had been studying the Bible together for most of the morning when Helen paused and asked, "What would you like to eat for lunch?"

I said, "I will eat anything; I am not picky. What would you like to eat?"

She said, "I'd like some vegetable soup from Brodie's," which was a little delicatessen not too far from her apartment.

I told her, "That sounds great!"

I thought we would drive to the restaurant and eat; that is not what happened. Helen took me by the hand and led me to the couch in her little den. We got down on our knees and she prayed, "Lord Jesus, we are here doing exactly what you want us to do today. You say in your word that 'We have not because we ask not,' (James 4:2 KJV) so Lord we would like some vegetable soup from Brodie's for lunch. Thank you so much for sending it! We love you Lord, in Jesus' name. Amen."

Hum, that was odd. I had never heard anyone pray like that before. We got up and went right back to study the Bible. Around 12:00 pm, there was a knock at the door. Helen looked at me, smiled, and opened the door. A friend of Helen's was standing there, holding a big, brown paper bag. She said, "Helen, I was driving by Brodie's a while ago and I thought you might like some vegetable soup. You know what, they gave me enough for two people!"

You could have picked my mouth up off of the floor! That was a life-changing moment for me. The Lord cares about providing vegetable soup? Really? In that one moment, everything that I thought I knew and believed about the Lord changed.

I had asked Jesus into my heart as a little girl, having grown up going to church. He was very much a part of my life, but at the same time, very far away. I knew He loved me, but perhaps other people needed God's help more than I did. My concerns seemed trivial compared to the troubles of others. I loved the Lord, but I did not really expect much from Him. I guess when it came to the Lord, I felt small; my relationship was not very personal. All that was about to change.

Helen Wright lived in Birmingham, Alabama, in a little, neat-as-a-pin, one-bedroom Redmont Gardens apartment in the Mountain Brooke area. She was seventy-two years old and I was twenty-seven when I met her. Helen was small-boned and thin; I felt I might break her if I hugged her too hard. She wore glasses that accentuated her lightly-colored, dancing hazel eyes; a beautiful soul was behind those eyes. Her hair was already more white than grey by then. Her teeth were not perfect, but she had a wonderful smile. She was always quick with an encouraging word.

There were only a handful of outfits in her closet, but she was proud of everything she owned. Helen told me that once she saw a lady wearing a gorgeous red coat and she said, "Lord, I would like a red coat just like that one." Later the next week, a young woman visited and gave her the same coat she had asked of the Lord. "See Misty," she said, "The Lord looks after my needs."

She was a truly gifted pianist. Her hands were small and as I watched her play many times, I wondered how she managed to stretch her fingers to reach the keys. Before retirement, she was a concert pianist and the featured pianist for the Birmingham Symphony. She taught fifteen years at the Conservatory of Music in Birmingham, Alabama, now Birmingham Southern College. In the summer she taught piano

16

at InterLocken, a music camp. She also taught piano at Southeastern Bible College. During that time she volunteered at Chalkville Juvenile Detention Center.

My twin sister Stormy had moved into the apartment across the hall from Helen. When I visited Stormy we awoke each morning to find an index card that Helen had pushed under the door. The card read, "Good morning! Come over for breakfast at 6:30. Today we will be having oatmeal, toast, juice, and coffee." Helen included a Bible verse and then covered the card with stickers. Helen loved stickers! What a wonderful way to start our days!

What was it about Helen? People were drawn to her. She was full of unconditional love and joy. It was contagious. Her personality lit up the world! I wanted to be around her. She seemed to know what I was thinking before I even said anything. She was gentle and kind. When some of the things that I needed to hear were not easy to communicate, she said, "You know I was reading in my Bible this morning…" She would then tell me what she had learned, but that wisdom was really meant for me. Those lessons always applied to my troubles at that particular time.

Helen talked to the Lord about every little thing. He was her best friend. Helen was plugged in to Jesus. She listened to him and studied His Word every day. She totally depended upon Him. Helen's prayers were answered in surprising ways. Stormy had told me that Helen had a direct line to God. I was beginning to believe it.

Helen said, "Jesus taught that He is the vine, we are the branches and the Father is the gardener." She then opened her Bible and read Jesus' words, *"If you remain in me and my words remain in you, ask whatever you wish, and it will be given to you. This is to my father's glory, that you bear much fruit, showing yourselves to be my disciples,"* *(John 15:7).*

I asked, "Miss Helen, what does that mean: *'If you remain in me and my words remain in you'*?"

She explained that the more time we spend reading the Bible, the more we will understand Jesus and grow in intimacy. Everything comes from that intimacy.

Helen made journaling and Bible study a priority. She taught me that to meditate on scripture is more than just memorizing it. Helen took a scripture and wrote it on an index card. She said it over and over, all the while talking to the Lord about it.

She inquired, "Lord, what does this mean?"

"How does this reveal who you are, your character, your nature or personality?"

"Is there a promise in it for me?"

"Is there something here for me because of what you have done?"

"How does this apply to my life now?"

"What am I to do with this information?"

She waited for divine revelation. When she received a truth, she wrote it down. She chewed on that scripture and processed it until it became a part of her. Responding biblically was her normal and first reaction. If she felt sick, she went to Jesus first. If she had a need, she turned to the Lord first. If she became fearful or defensive, she went back to her knees. She wrestled with the scripture until she could stand on it. Then, she added the "yes" and the "amen" to it!

The reading of scripture to Helen was not just a good idea. She surrendered herself totally and came into agreement with what it taught. "Lord, you promised it, it is for me and I believe it!" She applied this to everything in her life. Helen lived in a place of divine encounter. She drew on the reality in which she lived. Helen's very intimate relationship with Jesus enabled her to have heavenly, miraculous experiences.

If we believe that God will take care of us, we will go and do what he asks us to do. We must be sure what we believe. Without that knowledge there is no firm foundation for our faith. Our foundation as Christians is rooted in the life of Jesus Christ and in the Word of God.

Faith means putting our trust in something or someone; we will not have faith in someone we do not trust. The same is true for God. We will not have faith in God if we do not trust Him.

We can only give what we have received. Helen had a lifetime worth of receiving.

*Now to Him who is able to do exceeding abundantly above all
we_ask or think, according to the power that works in us...*
　　　　　　　　　　　　　　　—Ephesians 3:20, NKJV (emphasis mine)

Jesus can do infinitely more than we can <u>ask</u>, which is the reach of our prayer life. Jesus can do exceedingly more than we <u>think</u>, which is the reach of our imagination. I have a big imagination! Dreaming and imagination hold hands and skip together down the road toward faith. The older I get, the more imagination I have because I have seen countless answered prayers. I dream bigger than I ever have because I know God is faithful. I am filled with excitement and expectation! I call it having a Holy Spirit excitement. My expectation is so great, cheerleading routines are going on inside my spirit. Dream big! Pray big! I believe an outrageous bucket list thrills God!

It is important that we renew our minds with the Word of God because the renewed mind enhances faith. The un-renewed mind is at war with God. The Word says we must <u>believe with our heart</u> to be saved. It does not say we must believe with our minds. We must also confess with our <u>mouths</u> that we believe.

> *If you declare with your <u>mouth</u>, "Jesus is Lord," and <u>believe in</u>*
> *<u>your heart</u> that God raised him from the dead, you will be saved.*
> *<u>For it is with your heart that you believe</u> and are justified, and <u>it</u>*
> *<u>is with your mouth that you confess</u> and are saved.*
> *—Romans 10:9-10, NIV (emphasis mine)*

Faith does not come from the <u>mind</u>; it comes from the <u>heart</u>. If faith comes from the heart, why do I need to spend time studying the Bible? We must know the Word of God in order to move ourselves into an intimate relationship with Jesus and gain an understanding of how His Kingdom works here on earth. We should use this wisdom to make choices in our lives that will invite the presence of the Holy Spirit into our everyday reality. The more kingdom-minded we become, the more expectation we will have. We will have a fulfilling partnership with Jesus. We set feelings of unworthiness aside. We position ourselves to live in a place of divine encounter. We come into agreement with the Lord's way of doing things.

Our quest should be to deepen our encounter with the Lord Himself. There must be a divine encounter. When Helen opened her apartment door and the woman was standing there with vegetable soup, that was a divine encounter! How could Helen expect the Lord to answer her prayer for soup? She had invested hours, days, months and years in getting to know God and in studying His Word. Jesus had become her best friend. She knew Him and He knew her. She knew what He would do.

We cannot give what we do not have. We will never do the things we need to do if we do not have the wherewithal to do them. We will not trust Jesus to help us if we do not have faith in Him. We must fill our minds with the Word of God and then act upon it. We must grow in our relationship with Jesus and really take time to get to know Him.

Helen trusted Jesus implicitly, but never tried to talk me into believing her way. No, she was smarter than that. What she did was even more effective. She showed me her relationship with Jesus by letting me see Christ work in and through her life.

"Lord Jesus," she would say, "This morning I ask that you to be in charge today. You are the only one who knows what my day will be like. What should I wear?" Then she would take time and listen for His answer. Every decision she made was because of what the Lord told her, no matter how small it was.

Before I met Helen, I believed God cared only about the big things that happened in my life. I did not talk with Him about the little things. I was concerned that I might pray incorrectly or not know what to say. What if I asked for the wrong thing? I was not sure the Lord really cared, so I was not really into prayer. I had very low self-esteem. I did more of the emergency kind of prayer: "Lord, I have gone and done it again! Please come and save my bacon." Now who in the world would take me seriously? I was the poster child for the boring, non-effective Christian.

Helen had a victorious Christian life, but more than that it was adventurous and fun. Helen's intimate relationship with Jesus and her passionate risks of faith set her apart from everyone else. Every obstacle in her life became an opportunity for a miracle.

"Worrying is carrying tomorrow's load with today's strength- carrying two days at once. It is moving into tomorrow ahead of time. Worrying doesn't empty tomorrow of its sorrow, it empties today of its strength."
Corrie Ten Boom

One day, in a state of desperation I visited Helen. Nothing was going right in my life. She listened patiently as I talked about unexpected bills, unresolved conflicts, and troubles at work. Helen nodded occasionally as I prattled on about my frustrations. She let me finish and then immediately stood, threw her hands in the air and began praising the Lord. I was slightly offended at first and tried not to show it on my face.

Helen prayed, "Thank you, Lord! Oh thank you, Lord. Misty is in the perfect place in her life right now. She has so many needs. We are excited about it! Now we will be able to watch you answer her prayers. You are taking care of every detail in every situation. Nothing is too big for You! She is at the stepping off place to success. We trust you, Lord. In Your Name, amen."

I am not sure what I was expecting from her, but I definitely was not expecting that! Deep down I think I really wanted sympathy. I did not get any. It took a minute for me to process what she had said in the prayer. In that one moment, she had revealed my stinking thinking.

Just as I was sorting everything in my mind, she said, "This is exciting! Now let's talk to the Lord about every detail and let Him take care of it for us."

That is what we did. She got out some paper and I wrote it all down. She said, "I have lots of paper."

We surrendered everything to the Lord. I felt one hundred pounds lighter and was filled with peace. Sweet peace!

Casting the whole of your cares [all your anxieties, all your worries, all your concerns, once and for all] on Him, for He cares for you affectionately and cares about you watchfully.
—1 Peter 5:7, Amplified Bible

It was a wonderful experience! I really wanted to know and understand Helen's Jesus; the real Jesus, not the fabricated imposter I had created. I made up my mind that my relationship with Jesus was going to be one of complete trust.

I had been in church my whole life and had a lot of religious ideas. I heard:

"God doesn't answer prayer."

"There are no miracles today."

"You have to be good enough."

"Learn to live with that problem. It's just a thorn in your flesh"

"God wants people to suffer. It's for our own good."

In the short time that I had known Helen, I had learned that these things were not true. What a small God I was serving. I had let my problems become bigger than God. My prayers were feeble because, in my mind, my God was small. God is bigger than my biggest problem or my biggest need! I wanted to grow spiritually, and therefore, needed to be stretched. I wanted more! I was hungry to know all that Helen could teach. So I listened, watched, studied and learned. The Master had sent me a master.

I started thinking about it. The Lord knows everything about everyone and every situation. He also has the time, wisdom and unlimited resources to handle every detail. He loves me and wants the best for me. Why wouldn't I want to involve Him in what is going on in my life? Why wouldn't I want to let Him help me? My two choices: I can do everything by myself or I can trust the Lord to help me. That is a no brainer. I wanted to know more about the real Jesus. Could I really trust Him as Helen did? I was about to find out!

"I consider wisdom supernatural because it isn't taught by men - it's a gift from God."

—Joyce Meyer

Helen understood what I was going through. She had had the same fears and asked the same questions that I had been asking. She said, "Everyone has to grow in their own relationship with Jesus, just like we have to grow up in life. No baby comes out of the womb walking. It is a process. We learn about God, we learn about ourselves, and then we learn to make the journey together. He wants us to realize that we are important. Our presence on the earth is a divine appointment. We are supposed to be here and we have a divine purpose."

This was a learning process for me. I began talking to God about all of my problems, but I was not giving them to Him. I was not letting go. God gave me the wonderful gift of free will and He will not go against my will. If I choose to pick up a problem, He will let me carry it. He will let me carry that burden.

Helen made me feel a little better by telling me this story:

I taught piano for a time at South Eastern Bible College. Several of the students from SEBC volunteered and taught a Sunday school class at Chalkville Juvenile Detention Center. One day, their car broke down and they needed a ride. I drove them that day and every Sunday after that. I began volunteering and after my first year there, the students asked if I would teach a Bible class. I told them I taught piano, but I had never taught the Bible. I will have to pray and confirm that with the Lord. I had lunch that week with the president of South Eastern Bible College and his wife. I told them about the opportunity and asked their advice. They prayed and said, "We feel as though you are supposed to do it."

Inquisitive, I asked, "Were you seeking Godly council?"

"Yes, I was," she continued.

On the first day I read the class the scripture from John 14:12-14 (NIV) where Jesus said, *"I tell the truth, anyone who has faith in me will do what I have been doing. He will do even greater things than these, because I am going to the Father. And I will do whatever you ask in my name, so that the Son may bring glory to the Father. You may ask me for anything in my name, and I will do it."* I told the students how much God loved them and emphasized how much He wanted them to talk with Him about everything.

I told them that we should talk with Jesus about all of our cares and worries because He cares for us. We can trust Him. It is good to ask God for things. He wants to take care of us. I taught 1 Peter 5:6-7 (NIV): *"Humble yourselves, therefore, under God's mighty hand, that he may lift you up in due time. Cast all your anxiety on him because he cares for you."*

I asked, "Did they understand the scripture?"

Helen said, "Yes, as a matter of fact one young girl [we will call her Susie] lingered after the class and got my attention. Her eyes got very big, she sat up straight, and asked 'Does God really want me to ask Him for things?'"

Helen said, "Sure!"

Susie got excited and exclaimed, "Then let's pray and ask God for some red ballet slippers. I've always wanted a pair!"

Helen said, "I took her by her hands and we prayed and asked the Lord for the slippers."

As Helen was telling the story she paused for a moment. "Now Misty, to be honest, when she said red ballet slippers, I acted confident on the outside but on the inside I melted. My first thought was: Where in the world was I going to get red ballet slippers?"

I nodded, trying to imagine the younger Helen. She continued, "Now, that was during a time when there were no malls, and no computers to order from. Finding red ballet slippers was a real challenge! There was a Sears and Roebuck Store which had a catalogue that included ballet slippers, but none of them were red ones. I went to every place in Birmingham that I could think of and could not find any."

I was surprised that Helen even considered buying the slippers herself. I said, "Ms. Helen, you tried to answer Susie's prayer yourself?"

She said, "Yes, I did, but I could not find any slippers. The next week when we met for the class I could see the disappointment on her face when she realized that I did not have the red ballet slippers."

"Maybe you were hoping that someone else might give her a pair."

"No, no, I was really trying to answer her prayer myself."

Susie was impatient. "'Why didn't God bring the ballet slippers? Maybe you are not praying enough.'"

"At this point, Misty, I did not know what to do. I grabbed her hand one more time, we prayed together again."

Helen admitted, "I was so disappointed that I talked with the Lord about it later." Helen mimicked what she had done. She put her hands together, pointed her fingers upward and cast her eyes to heaven. "Now Lord, we cannot let this little girl down. She wants ballet slippers!"

"I tried to gather my faith," Helen said, "but the following week our prayer still was not answered. Susie was deflated and I was losing faith. But I reassured her, all the while wondering if it was not I that needed the reassurance."

"That's all right, Susie," I said, "we will pray and ask again! We are supposed to ask again. He will bring them!"

Helen was acting with as much confidence as she could muster. On the inside, however, she was having a crisis of faith. "Lord," she said, "you sent a novice to teach those students. They are not asking for spiritual things. This girl asked for red ballet slippers. If you do not bring them, then I am not teaching this class ever again. It is in the Book." Helen pointed to her Bible. "If what is in this Book is not true then I need to know. Susie is counting on you and you cannot let her down!"

Helen was emphatic. She had a mixture of emotions all at one time. She was afraid that God would not answer the prayer! What would she tell Susie? She could never teach Bible study again if they did not believe her. No, she could not do that! "I had decided that when I went back the following Sunday I would tell them that I was not going to teach the class anymore."

I was listening very intently now.

Helen continued:

When Sunday came I got the surprise of my life! Susie came skipping, smiling, and giggling down the hall. There, swinging in her hand, were the red ballet slippers! I was so shocked I blurted, "Where did you get those slippers?"

In a flash Susie explained, "Why, Jesus gave them to me of course, Ms. Helen. Didn't you know? I want to know this Jesus. He answers prayers! Will you help me ask Jesus to come into my heart?"

Susie grabbed my hand, pulled me to the piano bench and said, "Let's pray." She is the first person I ever led to the Lord and she really did it herself! The red ballet slippers came in the mail without a return address or a note and we never knew who sent them. Can you beat that?

Helen kept teaching the class!

"How can a person deal with anxiety? You might try what one fellow did. He worried so much that he decided to hire someone to do his worrying for him. He found a man who agreed to be his hired worrier for a salary of $200,000 per year. After the man accepted the job, his first question to his boss was, 'Where are you going to get $200,000 per year?' To which the man responded, 'That's your worry.'"

Max Lucado

Too often we feel just as Helen did. Uncertainty leads to a faith that waivers. How do we know when we have completely surrendered a problem to the Lord? First, we will not come up with a contingency plan. In other words, we should not be thinking, "If the Lord doesn't answer my prayer, then I will solve my own problem." If I needed money and my prayer was not immediately answered, for example, I should not reach for the phone to call Uncle Fred and ask him for a loan.

Secondly, when we have surrendered our problems to the Lord, a peace will settle over us. We will experience a peace that passes understanding (Philippians 4:7). God will give us <u>peace</u> even in the middle of our storms.

> *You will keep him in perfect <u>peace</u>, whose mind is stayed on You, because he trusts in You.*
> *—Isaiah 26:3, NKJV (emphasis mine)*

> *[Jesus said] <u>Peace</u> I leave with you; my <u>peace</u> I give you. I do not give to you as the world gives. Do not let your hearts be troubled and do not be afraid.*
> *—John 14:27, NIV (emphasis mine)*

Once I had given all of my problems to the Lord, I felt peaceful. It was a wonderful experience! I made up my mind that my relationship with Jesus was going to be one of complete trust. First, I had to correct my thinking.

"The size of a challenge should never be measured by what we have to offer. It will never be enough. Furthermore, provision is God's responsibility, not ours. We are merely called to commit what we have - even if it's no more than a sack lunch."
Charles R. Swindoll

Chapter Two

A Birthday Cake, a Veil and a Get Out of Jail Free Card

"For what you see and hear depends a good deal on where you are standing: it also depends on what sort of person you are."

C. S. Lewis, *The Magician's Nephew*

Each time I visited Helen I came away encouraged and motivated. I realized I knew *about* the Lord, but I did not really know Him. I did not trust Him. I was determined to study the Word and get to know Jesus.

I asked, "Helen, when you say 'relationship,' what do you mean?"

Helen said, "Having a relationship is about sharing. The more you get to know one another, the more you trust each other."

I asked, "Doesn't He already know everything about us?"

She laughed and said, "Sure He does! He wants us to talk with Him about everything, anyway. Besides, we do not have to worry about saying anything wrong because He already knows everything. It makes it easy."

I said, "Ms. Helen, the Lord is not tangible. I cannot wrap my arms around Him and give Him a hug. I cannot sit across a table from Him, look into His eyes and talk to Him. It is so frustrating."

Helen smiled and said, "I know what you mean, but you will get the hang of it. Pretty soon you will hear Him very clearly, and He will fill you with so much love you will think you might pop!"

I knew she was right because I had experienced a little of that. Helen knew that He loved her completely and because of that she stepped out in faith. I made up my mind to trust the Lord with everything, too. Well, I would try to, anyway.

A couple of weeks later I received an unexpected bill in the mail; it was something I thought I had taken care of, but apparently had overlooked. Now the bill had come due. You guessed it! I did not have the money to pay it. So I followed Helen's example and put my case before the Lord. "Lord, please forgive me for not taking care of this as I should have. I really messed up, because now I do not have the money to pay this bill. I watched as you provided for Helen. Lord, thank you for providing for me."

Some time passed and I still had not received the money. A letter came in the mail scolding me about my credit. My faith began to waver. I came up with my own solution. I would apply for a credit card and then pay the bill with that. It was not a very wise thing to do. I felt good about getting the creditor off of my back, but my contingency plan left me saddled with a credit card bill and interest. This, by the way, was not in my budget. I had enslaved myself to this little piece of plastic!

I went back to the Lord and prayed, "Lord, I feel like an idiot. I gave in to fear and did not trust you. Please forgive me. I took things into my own hands and tried to solve the problem myself. I am still in a mess. Please meet this need and provide the money. In Jesus' name, amen."

Yes, I was begging. Where was my faith? The Lord understood what I was going through. I heard Helen's voice in my head, "Faith grows one step at a time." A couple of days later, I received a check and a note in the mail from a friend who was completely unaware of my situation. She said, "The Lord let me know that you needed money." The check was the exact amount of the original bill. Praise God! I paid off the credit card, everything except the finance charges. If I had only waited on the Lord! Talk about learning the hard way.

When I told Helen what had happened, she encouraged me by telling me another story. Helen began:

Years ago a student in my Bible study came to talk with me. She witnessed the answered prayer when the Lord provided the red ballet slippers.

The girl said, "Ms. Helen, is that true that the Lord will answer anyone's prayer?"

I said, "Why yes, it is."

The girl asked, "Would you pray with me, please? Sunday is my birthday and I would like a birthday cake. I have never had a birthday cake."

Helen explained that the girl had come from a broken home and the family was very poor.

Helen said, "Of course I will!"

So I took the girls hands into mine and prayed and asked the Lord to send her a cake. The girl grinned, squealed and then went on her way.

I thought to myself, now <u>this</u> I can do! I ordered a cake from the bakery with white icing, a big red bow and large roses done in fancy sugar. The next Sunday I proudly walked the cake down the hallway and into the classroom.

When the girl saw the cake she said, "Oh, Ms. Helen, where is your faith? That is the third birthday cake I have gotten this week!'

I laughed along with Helen! "Lesson learned. Don't waste time and money doing something that the Lord can do better! Am I right?"

Helen, still smiling, replied, "That's right! Even more than that, I learned to surrender everything to God. I learned not only to trust him with the things that I cannot do myself, but also with the things that I can do for myself. I learned to trust Him with literally everything! Can you beat that?"

She had her focus on Jesus; she looked at things from His perspective. They had the strongest and most miraculous relationship that I had ever seen! I realized that I had been doing exactly the opposite. My focus was almost entirely on myself. I was selfishly looking at things from my perspective. Where is the faith in that? I almost always had a contingency plan. Nothing ever worked out the way I thought it would. Over and over again, I felt like a failure and became intensely introspective. It was like looking into a mirror and only noticing my inadequacies and failures. I begin to justify my erroneous behavior. Was I good enough? Did the Lord really love me? Did I pray enough?

My works mentality compelled me to believe I had to perform to be accepted. I was like a dog chasing its tail—around and around I went. I was in bondage and did not know it! The Lord had never rejected me, but I was acting as though He had.

The enemy, Satan, likes for us to put our focus on ourselves. That becomes a trap. We will reproduce the things that we focus on. What we see is what we will become. If we focus on our inadequacies, we will talk ourselves into a deep depression. It is as though we have a veil over our heads. Instead of moving forward in life, we are stuck. Satan laughs!

When Moses came down from Mount Sinai with the Ten Commandments, his face glowed from being in God's presence (Exodus 34:29-35). Moses put a veil over his face to keep the people from being terrified by the brightness of his face.

> *Therefore, since we have such hope, we use great boldness of speech—unlike Moses, who put a veil over his face so that the children of Israel could not look steadily at the end of what was passing away. But their minds were blinded. For until this day the same veil remains unlifted in the reading of the Old Testament, because the veil is taken away in Christ. But even to this day, when Moses is read, a veil lies on their heart. Nevertheless when one turns to the Lord, the veil is taken away. Now the Lord is the Spirit; and where the Spirit of the Lord is, there is liberty. But we all, with open face beholding as in a glass the glory of the Lord, are changed into the same image from glory to glory, [even] as by the Spirit of the Lord.*
> *—2 Corinthians 3:12-18, NKJV (emphasis mine)*

The apostle Paul suggests that the veil illustrates the fading of an old system and the veiling of the hearts and minds of the people and their refusal to repent. Whenever we turn our hearts to Christ, the veil is removed. When we surrender, understanding comes. It does not say the veil is removed and then we believe. My heart is capable of a response that my mind does not yet understand. It is through surrender that He provides freedom from sin and condemnation.

Therefore, there is now no condemnation for those who are in Christ Jesus...

—*Romans 8:1, NIV*

God convicts, but never condemns. To convict means to find someone guilty. God will pardon us if we ask for forgiveness—a "Get Out of Jail Free" card, if you will. When we sin, we are miserable. God's forgiveness brings peace. We are then encouraged to do better the next time. We have learned that He will be there to help us.

Condemnation, however, is totally different. If a sign placed on a building says, "Condemned," it means the building is worthless and about to be torn down. This is how Satan wants us to feel. Condemnation is one of the tools that Satan uses. He wants us to be so full of shame that we will not go to the Lord. If Satan can keep us from trusting God, he has crippled us! We must learn the difference between condemnation and conviction. If we give in to feelings of condemnation, we are giving Satan authority over our lives. We should take back our God-given authority over Satan.

Jesus removes the heavy burden from our trying to please Him and our guilt for failing to do so. He loves us, accepts us, and forgives us. If we focus on Jesus, it is liberating! Those who feel condemned by God will never have faith to trust Him.

"And Grace calls out, 'You are not just a disillusioned old man who may die soon, a middle-aged woman stuck in a job and desperately wanting to get out, a young person feeling the fire in the belly begin to grow cold. You may be insecure, inadequate, mistaken or potbellied. Death, panic, depression, and disillusionment may be near you. But you are not just that. You are accepted.' Never confuse your perception of yourself with the mystery that you really are accepted."

Brennan Manning, The Ragamuffin Gospel:
Good News for the Bedraggled,
Beat-Up, and Burnt Out

Chapter Three

A WEDDING DRESS, ORPHANS AND SALTINE CRACKERS

"You are loved by your maker not because you try to please him and succeed, or fail to please him and apologize, but because he wants to be your father."
Max Lucado

Our struggle with condemnation and temptation really becomes difficult when we give our lives to Christ. The struggle was not as difficult before we got saved because we were living for ourselves, the center of our universe, dominated by the desires of the flesh. The wrestling is actually evidence that we have been born again. Dead men do not wrestle. We struggle with our fallen nature because it has memory and still has desires and appetites.

"Yes, reason has been a part of organized religion, ever since two nudists took dietary advice from a talking snake."
Jon Stewart

These things in our nature are there from a very young age. We do not naturally know God at birth. We lost that at the fall. That is why we have been given the right to become <u>children of God</u> and receive His nature.

But as many as received Him, to them He gave the right to become <u>children of God</u>, to those who believe in His name: who were born, not of blood, nor of the will of the flesh, nor of the will of man, but of God.

—John 1:12-13 (emphasis mine)

If you have ever taken care of a baby, you know that everything is all about them. They learn how to manipulate and cry in order to get what they want when they are only a few months old. They will get you out of bed in the middle of the night. It does not matter how tired you are, there is no mercy. They know what to do to coax a bottle or pacifier out of you. When they get a little older, their favorite words are, "me," "mine," "no," and, "I want to do it myself!" Oh yes, that selfish nature is there!

If you are wondering what the "desires of the flesh" really are, there is a list of them in Galatians 5. Among them are sexual immorality, impurity, lust, hatred, discord, jealousy, anger, selfish ambition, arrogance, envy, lying, stealing, wild living, cheating, and greed. When tempted, the Holy Spirit will encourage us to turn away from these things. We then have to decide if we are going to listen to the Holy Spirit and walk away, or give in to the flesh.

When we were saved, a new nature took up residence inside of us and is dominating our hearts. We have been given everything we need to live a <u>Godly life</u>. If we give in to the flesh, however, we feel unworthy. We do not believe we are good enough for God to answer our prayers. That is absolutely true! <u>We are not good enough</u> and we will never be good enough, no matter how hard we try. Thankfully, we do not have to be good enough.

There is no one righteous, not even one; there is no one who understands; there is no one who seeks God. All have turned

*away, they have together become worthless, there is <u>no one who
does good,</u> not even one.*

> *—Romans 3:11-12, NIV (emphasis mine)*

*There is not a righteous man on earth who <u>does what is right</u>
and never sins.*

> *—Ecclesiastes 7:20, NIV (emphasis mine)*

What standards are we trying to live up to? Who sets the standards?
What is the grading scale? The American culture encourages success.
We encourage our children to be successful, to make good grades, to
get a good education, and to live "The American Dream." We are
pressured to measure up.

It complicates things, however, when we place the same expectations
on our spiritual lives. We are "accepted in the beloved," (Ephesians 1:6,
KJV). God has already accepted us. We do not have to earn anything
from God. It is impossible. We cannot earn what has been freely given.
God loves us just the way we are. We do not have to worry about
getting an "F" on our spiritual report card. There is no report card.
We do not have to be afraid of making mistakes with Him. Jesus took
care of that for us. There is forgiveness. It takes the pressure off. We
should want to do things God's way because we are in a relationship
with Jesus. We love Him and He loves us. He knows what is best. We
should not do things because we are afraid we are going to disappoint
Him. We should not allow Satan to make us feel guilty. We do not have
to perform to be accepted. We have already been accepted; "<u>We have
been justified through faith</u>."

*Therefore, since <u>we have been justified through faith</u>, we have
peace with God through our Lord Jesus Christ, through whom
we have gained access by faith into this grace in which we now
stand. And we rejoice in the hope of the glory of God.*

> *—Romans 5:1-2, NIV (emphasis mine)*

We are now in right standing with God. We have been justified and
made righteous. Justified (just-if-I'd) simply means "it is just if I had"

never sinned. In other words, God looks at it (sin) and us as though we are completely forgiven. It is just if we had never sinned.

The gift (of right standing with God) is not like the trespass (the sin Adam committed <u>which condemned all men</u>).

Therefore, just as sin entered the world through one man, and death through sin, and in this way <u>death came to all men</u>, because all sinned...
—Romans 5:12, NIV (emphasis mine)

I was blessed to meet Danny and Brenda, a couple who put their past regrets aside, prayed from their hearts, and stepped out in faith. They were a part of a Transitional Housing Ministry at The Ark in Panama City Beach, Florida where I volunteered. Danny, Brenda and I were writing down a few obtainable goals that they wanted to work toward. They had recently been homeless and living under a tarp in the woods not too far from The Ark. They had been through our screening process and were a part of our transitional housing program.

I was finishing up their list and asked, "Okay, we have your long and short term goals. Is there anything else you would like to ask the Lord to help you do?"

Danny said, without hesitation, "We would like to get married." Danny and Brenda had been a couple for many years, but had never married. They had been going to Gulf Beach Baptist Church since they moved to the area and were growing in their relationship with the Lord. Marriage was now very important to them.

I said, "Marriage! That, I am sure the Lord will help you do." We had no idea how we would make this happen and no money to do it with either. So we began praying. We talked with the people at their church and they happily agreed to help us. Before long we got a call letting us know we could use their church for the ceremony and that someone had volunteered to bake a wedding cake. Someone offered to take wedding pictures. Someone else offered to make refreshments. One of the pastors helped them get a marriage license and he promised to marry them. A wedding date was set and we were well on our way. What would we do about a wedding dress for Brenda and a suit for Danny? Word began to spread and we received a call from someone from the Catholic church's John Lee Thrift Store. There was a wedding dress there that might do. Brenda and I were praying all the way there that the dress would fit and that she would love it.

Brenda asked, "Is it all right if I pray for some flowers with a little blue in them and maybe some blue shoes? Is that silly that I want blue shoes?"

I said, "Of course that's not silly! Brenda, the Lord loves you and wants to bless you. Ask Him; He knows your heart anyway." So we asked the Lord to bless her. We followed one of the ladies to the back room of the thrift store and she pulled down an heirloom box. When the box was opened, we could barely contain our excitement. Inside was a gorgeous designer wedding gown that had been made in Paris, France. It fit her like it was made for her. Brenda loved it!

In no time a lady found another box with a bouquet with little blue flowers, and a garter with a little blue ribbon and bow. Tears welled up in Brenda's eyes. She was overwhelmed.

I called a friend who attended Woodlawn United Methodist Church. I thought she might have a pair of shoes that would fit Brenda. She called another friend and in no time we had the perfect pair of blue shoes. We found a second-hand Brooks Brothers suit that Danny loved and a pair of shoes for him. The suit cost five dollars. Someone from Woodlawn Church donated a hotel room on the beach for their honeymoon. I am happy to say that Danny and Brenda had the sweetest little wedding, complete with special music. As I write this, they both have good jobs and are nearing their goal of saving enough money to have a place of their own. God is so faithful!

Someone at the wedding pulled me aside and said, "This is what The Ark is all about isn't it?"

I asked, "What do you mean?"

She said, "The Methodist, Baptists and Catholics all pulled together to make this wedding happen. It is really remarkable. It is exactly what you said you guys at The Ark were working toward, pulling the community together!"

God looks beyond our difficulties and our bad decisions and sees a future and a hope.

God accepts us, even in our mess. When a child throws his food and makes a mess, do we stop loving that child? Of course not! God does not stop loving us either, no matter how big a <u>mess</u> we make of our lives. The trouble is we really feel badly when we mess up, don't we?

> *I do not understand what I do. For what I want to do I do not do, but <u>what I hate I do</u>. And if I do what I do not want to do, I agree that the law is good.*
>
> —*Romans 7:15, NIV (emphasis mine)*

Satan pushes us toward living under the law, but because of what Jesus sacrificed we can now live under grace. Let me explain what living under the law looks like. We know what we need to do (or not to do), but we do not do it (or do it anyway). Then we feel guilty and condemned. So we turn to God, acknowledge our need and try as hard as we can to be good. We fail and then feel miserable. At the end of the day we pray for forgiveness and God empties our bucket of sins. The next day we fill our bucket with sin again and the cycle starts all over. Then one day we go to heaven. What a terribly frustrating way to live! We do not have to live that way.

"Grace is not simply leniency when we have sinned. Grace is the enabling gift of God not to sin. Grace is power, not just pardon."

—John Piper,
*The Pleasures of God:
Meditations on God's Delight in Being God*

Where does the law come from? How do we know what we are supposed to do? What laws or rules are we always breaking? The law could actually be any law; there are laws written in the Bible. When we break these laws we call it sin. Noah Webster, in the first dictionary written in 1828 defines sin as "any voluntary transgression of the divine law, or violation of a divine command; a wicked act; or iniquity."

Similarly, the laws of society and the expectations of others also bind us. We faced this each day as children growing up and going to school. Confronted with peer pressure, we grouped ourselves into cliques in order to feel a sense of belonging. We labeled ourselves: the jocks, the nerds, the Goths, the drama geeks, the cheerleaders, or the outcasts. Everyone worked to fit in. We do this as adults as well.

Within our families there are rules. "Never visit anyone without an invitation," or "Do not tell anyone about your father's drinking problem," or "Don't call anyone after 8:00 p.m. That is rude."

There is even an internal law that guides what we should or should not do. Oh, and let us not forget about the laws we place on ourselves.

"I'm going to exercise three times each week."

"I'm going to only eat vegetables and fruit."

"I'm going to be nice to my neighbor who is always mean to me."

Do we really stick to these things? Even when we were not Christians we had an internal sense of what we should do, but we did not do it. It is as though two people reside in each of us. We know what to do to be a better father or husband, mother or daughter, aunt or friend, but instead <u>we do what we should not do or do not do what we should do.</u>

You see, at just the right time, when we were still <u>powerless,</u>
Christ died for the <u>ungodly</u>.
—Romans 5:6, NIV (emphasis mine)

The "powerless" part of that scripture is what we are talking about. This thing we want to do, the thing we need to do, is often the very thing that we cannot or will not do. <u>We feel powerless</u>. When Jesus died for us, we were given power. Satan, however, wants us to feel powerless and live in guilt and shame!

When I was a missionary in Africa, I heard a story of a young boy who felt powerless yet met his Goliath and prevailed. This story has been told and retold, and passed down from generation to generation.

It was a normal, hot and dusty day in Africa when a stranger came for a visit. A young village boy was fascinated by him and began to follow him around. The man told stories about Jesus and the boy was mesmerized. The man told the boy that he could know Jesus. He answered all of the boy's questions. He prayed with him. The boy's heart was filled with love. He came to have a relationship with Jesus.

The boy felt the presence of God and was so excited that he went straight to his hut to tell his family. He wanted them to know about this love.

"Father, I met a man and he told me the stories of Jesus. Can I teach you about Jesus?"

His father responded with a gruff, "No!" They would not listen. The boy prayed and asked God to show him what he needed to do.

All of his family worshipped idols. In the hut were seven idols sitting like statues in a row. They were carved out of wood and lined up from the biggest to the smallest. One was much bigger than the others.

One day the family had to go away for a while. The father asked the boy to stay home to prepare the food sacrifice for the idols. He was to put the food on the plates according to size and then to set the plates on the floor in front of each idol.

The boy did just as his father had instructed. All the while he was praying that Jesus would help his family to stop worshipping the idols. At that moment he had an idea. He got an axe and chopped every idol up except the largest one. Then he prayed and prayed as he waited for his family to come back home.

When his dad walked into the hut and saw the idols were destroyed, he was very angry, "What have you done to the idols?"

The boy said, "Father, it was the most amazing thing I have ever seen. I prepared the food just as you told me to and just as I was placing the plate in front of the largest idol he rose up and destroyed the rest of the idols!"

The father's face turn bright red and he yelled at the boy, "You are lying. The idol could not have done that. Where are his eyes that he could see? Where are his hands? Where are his feet? He cannot move! He could not have done it!"

The boy quietly said, "Father, if the idols do not have eyes so they cannot see; if they do not have ears so they cannot hear; if they do not have hands or feet so they cannot move; if they do not have a mouth so they cannot eat; what can they do? If they can do nothing, why are you worshiping them?"

The father paused, searching his brain for an answer. There was none. He was at a loss for words.

The boy continued, "Father, let me tell you about someone who is alive and who loves you and who will really help you! His name is Jesus."

The boy eventually led his entire family to the Lord.

No, we are not perfect, but we are not powerless either. What does Paul mean when he says that we are "un-God-ly"? We are not perfect as God is perfect. We all are sinners. For years I chased the elusive goal of becoming a perfect, Godly Christian. I compared myself to other spiritual giants who were accomplishing great things. I felt like a worm. I rolled around in self-pity and martyred myself on the hill of my own self-interests. I was never satisfied and complained about everything. I went to church and learned, but I was a miserable person that others did not want to be around. Instead of embracing the unconditional love and acceptance of Jesus, I kicked Him off the throne of my heart. I had to adjust my way of thinking.

We must look at ourselves differently. Our perspective must change.

We were all born in Adam. When we become Christians we are taken out of Adam and we are placed into Christ.

We were therefore buried with him through baptism into death in order that, just as Christ was raised from the dead through the glory of the father, we too may live a new life.
—Romans 6:4, NIV (emphasis mine)

In other words, all the benefits that were given to us through Christ's death and resurrection were given because we are in Him. We were taken out of Adam and out of condemnation and placed into Christ's peace and joy. Not only does that apply after we die, but it also applies in this life.

But Christ has indeed been raised from the dead, the first fruits of those who have fallen asleep. For since death came through a man, the resurrection of the dead comes also through a man. For as in Adam all die, so in Christ all will be made alive.
—1 Corinthians 15:20-22, NIV (emphasis mine)

41

Once we come into God's grace, we have taken off the old and put on the new. Imagine wearing dirty, ugly clothes that do not fit. Imagine, too, that negative, condemning and critical words such as *shame, guilt, fear, condemnation, ridicule, negativity, hatred* and *judgment* are imprinted all over the clothes. We are weighed down and hopeless. We strive to change, but those awful, negative labels hang on. We feel helpless.

Then we meet Jesus. He says, "Take off those old clothes. I have clothes made perfectly for you. In the pockets you will find everything needed to live an abundant life: joy, kindness, forgiveness, peace, patience, self-control and unconditional love," (Galatians 5:22-23). When we dress in these glorious and beautiful clothes we feel fresh, renewed! We then see ourselves differently.

> *If we have been <u>united with him like this in his death</u>, we will certainly also be united with him in his resurrection.*
> —*Romans 6:5, NIV (emphasis mine)*

What is true of Christ is true of us. <u>He was crucified and we are in Him</u>. Paul says we were crucified with Him. We go to heaven because we are in Christ. We live a different kind of life now because we are in Christ. Sin is not our master.

Some time ago I had the privilege of going with a mission team to Mexico. While there I spent time helping in an orphanage. The cinder block building was too small for the many children who lived there. The room for the babies was overcrowded and two, sometimes three, babies were in each crib. The place was severely understaffed. Three women struggled to care for all of the children. The room was never quiet; babies cried because they were hungry, needed changing, and wanted to be held. It was heart breaking. While we were there, we held and loved as many babies as we could.

In other rooms, children slept on makeshift cots or on the floor. The yard was dirt; the bottoms of little feet had long worn the grass away. We told stories about Jesus and hugged as many as we could. At the end of the day we took the children behind the building and bathed each one using a water hose. After they had dripped dry we pulled very used, but clean clothes out of a large cardboard box and dressed them. In the afternoon we all gathered under the shade of a big tree. The children sat on planks of wood, fashioned for benches, which surrounded the base of the tree. Dinner was served. Each child received a cup of water and one section of a saltine cracker, smeared with something that looked like potted meat. That is all they had.

An American student, heartbroken by the meager meal, stopped an ice cream vender peddling by on his bicycle. She dug deep into her pocket and bought every child an ice cream. The children were elated. It felt like the generosity of Christmas morning. I wondered if any of the children would ever be adopted out of the orphanage and taken to loving homes. What would it be like for them if they were?

Living in the grace of God is like international adoption. A child lives in an orphanage and by the rules of the orphanage, institution and law. The rules and laws completely dictate that child's life. Then, with a stroke of a pen, a legal transaction is made that goes beyond what the child wants or understands. That child goes from being an orphan to becoming a family member. He is given a new name. The child goes from poverty to wealth. He goes from having a little food to having plenty of food. He begins to take ownership in things. Everything is changed. The orphanage staff, agency, government, state or country loses authority over the child. They can show up at the door and the parents can say, "No, you have no authority over this child anymore." Everything has changed.

The older a child is the longer it takes for him to get used to this new love, family, surroundings, or school. I have a friend who adopted a child from an orphanage similar to the one in which I had volunteered. That child was given her very own room, new clothes and all the food she could eat. Yet, she would hide food under the bed in her room. Although she had been given everything she needed, she still behaved as though she was living in the orphanage.

We are like that young girl. Whether we recognized it or not, whether anyone told us or not, when we were taken out of Adam we got a new name, a new identity, a new family, and new destiny. Even better than that, sin lost its authority over us. We may have been saying yes to sin and wrestling within ourselves our entire lives, but sin is not our master.

"The law points you to self-efforts. Grace points you to the finished work of Jesus Christ."
—John Paul Warren

When we wrestle with sin or temptation, with which side of the argument do we identify? The "I shouldn't but I want to" side?

I have enough credit card debt as it is, but I want another pair of shoes.

I want to go there, but know I shouldn't go. But I really want to go.

I want to turn on the television, but I shouldn't. I have more important things to do.

I need to walk away from this video game, but I don't want to.

I need to close this web site. I shouldn't be looking at this, but I don't want to close it.

When we are in that "I shouldn't but I want to" frame of mind, with which side do we identify? Which side are we on?

When we wrestle with sin, do we wrestle from the standpoint of being an Adam? Do arguments sound something like this:

> *"Well, nobody is perfect."*
> *"I was raised in that kind of home."*
> *"I've always been susceptible to this."*
> *"My mom had this issue and her mom had this issue."*
> *"I can't help it."*
> *"This is the way women are."*
> *"All men are alike."*
> *"This is normal."*
> *"What do you expect?"*
> *"Everyone does it."*
> *"I deserve it."*
> *"This is natural."*
> *"This is just what people my age do."*
> *"I am a sinner."*

When we argue this way, we are arguing from the standpoint of sin. Our former selves are arguing. We will lose every time because we have identified with someone we are not. Somehow we have separated ourselves from the goodness and the righteousness of God. We have come into agreement with sin.

Life is completely different when we identify with who we are when we place ourselves in Christ. When we identify with Christ, our arguments will be something like this:

"Overeating is trying to rule me."

"Jealousy is trying to conquer me."

"Pornography still has power over me."

"Anger is ruling my life."

In the shadow of sin is death. I have had enough death in my life. I have eaten enough! I have been jealous enough! I have been consumed with porn long enough! I am tired of being angry! Why would anyone who is free from sin continue to live in it? Why would we embrace something that will continue to hurt us? Christ died for our sins and we are in Christ. He died once and for all and we are a part of that once and for all.

When we struggle and find ourselves in that raging battle of, "Oh, here comes that temptation again," we choose a side of the equation. The side that we identify with has everything to do with the outcome. As long as we identify with who we used to be, we will always behave the way we have always behaved.

> *Therefore <u>do not let sin reign</u> in your mortal body so that you obey its evil desires. Do not offer the parts of your body to sin, as an instrument of wickedness, but rather offer yourselves to God, as those who have been brought from death to life; and offer the parts of your body to him as instruments of righteousness. For sin shall not be your master, because you are not under the law, but under grace.*
> —*Romans 6:12-14, NIV (emphasis mine)*

Paul says, "Therefore <u>do not let</u>..." because we have a choice. We can say no to sin because Jesus has broken the power of sin. We are in a new family. Sin can knock on the door, ring the doorbell, text us, e-mail us, call us, or friend us but we have the power to say, *"Get behind me, Satan! You are a stumbling block to me; you do not have in mind the concerns of God, but merely human concerns," (Matthew 16:23).* Eyes, you will not look at things that you should not look at or that are degrading to others. Feet, you will not carry me to places I do not need to go. Hands, you will not pick up, buy, carry, or do anything dishonest. Mind, you will keep your thoughts pure.

God will help us battle stubborn sin. A pastor in Africa told me a story about a woman who was a member of his congregation. Her husband was an alcoholic and difficult to live with when he was drinking. In the Ghanaian culture, if you disobey your husband, he can kick you out of the house. You and all of your children will be left with nothing and no place to live. It has happened many times and the women live in fear. Their culture has enslaved them. God always provides a way out.

This faithful woman's husband was not a Christian. He went to the places where alcohol was sold and stayed there for long periods of time. She grew very weary of it. One day as she was praying, the still small voice of the Lord whispered to her and she knew what she needed to do. She cleaned the house and made everything nice. She cooked his favorite food. When he came home he sat down to eat and she said, "You know that I love you very much, I really do. I want you to be happy. But there is one thing that you do that really bothers me. If you really love me you will let me tell you about it."

He sat up a little bit in his chair and said, "I love you, too. What is it?"

This was her opportunity. She said, "I know how you like to drink and that's fine, but you are gone most of the time and I never see you. I don't like it when you are away. I miss you. Let me ask you a question: How much alcohol do you think you drink in a week?"

He proudly said, "Seven liters!"

She said, "Great! I will buy seven liters of your favorite drink and I will keep it at home. When you want to drink, instead of going somewhere else, you can just buy it from me, here at home."

He thought about it and said, "All right, that sounds like a good idea."

The woman purchased the alcohol, just as she said she would. Then she placed her hands on the bottles and began to pray over them. She prayed that the alcohol would not mean anything to her husband anymore and that his desire for it would go away. She prayed that he would give his life to the Lord Jesus. All during the week she paid him good attention and he drank the alcohol. She kept praying. When the next week came she asked, "How much alcohol would you like for me to purchase this week?"

He said, "One liter."

He finished drinking the bottle on a Saturday and looked at is wife and said, "I think I would like to go to church with you tomorrow."

She was overjoyed! He had never been to church with her before. After the service she began to introduce him by saying, "This is my husband and he is visiting today," but that is not what happened. Just as she said, "This is my husband and he is..." he interrupted her and said, "Yes, I am her husband but I am not just visiting here today. I want to know about this Jesus Christ."

Right there on that spot he became a Christian. He repented for his sins, stopped drinking and has been faithfully coming to church every Sunday.

Thank God for the prayers of a faithful wife. Yes, the Holy Spirit empowers us and brings us to a place of repentance. We should repent for our own sin. We should repent for hurting others. When we feel sorrow and deep contrition for what we have done, God changes our hearts. We are then one step closer to the restoration of relationships. True repentance makes restoration possible. God's grace is absolutely necessary to bring healing. Healing cannot come without the grace of God. Restoration for a believer means we should work toward restoration of relationships. Restoration is defined by what Jesus did on the cross. *"Dear friends, since God so loved us..."* that is, if God was so willing to protect His relationship with us, instead of protecting our relationship with His rules *"...we also ought to love one another,"* *(1 John 4:11, NIV)*. God does not want something <u>from</u> you; He wants something <u>for</u> you! We have to take responsibility. What is the bottom line when it comes to law and grace? Law leads to rules, judgment, and a works mentality. Grace leads to forgiveness and love, which empowers our faith.

"But if I've learned anything about the world of grace, it's that failure is always a chance for a do-over."
—Brennan Manning,
All Is Grace: A Ragamuffin Memoir

Chapter Four

A Muslim, Salt and a Pocketknife

"We, the public, are easily, lethally offended. We have come to think of taking offence as a fundamental right. We value very little more highly than our rage, which gives us, in our opinion, the moral high ground. From this high ground we can shoot down at our enemies and inflict heavy fatalities. We take pride in our short fuses. Our anger elevates, transcends."
—Salman Rushdie, *East, West*

When someone hurts or takes advantage of us, it offends us. When an offense is committed, we become angry. We feel justified in withholding our love. The person who offended us broke the rules, after all. They have sinned and are unworthy of love. They deserve to be punished. When we withhold our love, anxiety fills the void, and a spirit of fear directs our behavior toward the offender. Feeling offended may even direct our behavior toward God.

"Some people take offense like it's a limited time offer."
—Tim Fargo

When we are afraid, we want to control. Our response to the sin of other people is to adopt a set of controls that help us feel as though we are still in charge. That is why the typical practice in a family, church, or government is to require an offender to be punished in order to prove that the family, church or government is still in charge. In doing so, we help to confirm the belief that the offender is powerless to change and take responsibility for his behavior. Our justification sounds something like this:

> *"You have offended me."*
> *"You broke the rules and failed."*
> *"You deserve to be punished."*
> *"I don't love you anymore."*
> *"I am overwhelmed with anxiety."*
> *"I must gain control."*
> *"I will make you prove you are worthy."*

In a rule driven environment, we do not feel someone is repentant unless they apologize and are punished in some way. The root issue that led that person to sin is never dealt with because we never get to that place of love. We want them to jump through hoops in order to prove themselves to us. When we demand this kind of justice we are allowing ourselves to be driven by what society expects. We are not allowing the light of God to shine into the darkness.

"A day without sunshine is like, you know, night."
—Steve Martin

I mentioned that I worked as a missionary for a time in Ghana, West Africa. The pastors I worked with welcomed, and appreciated, short-term missionaries who came from other countries to help us teach, preach, plant churches or work in the villages. We made the long trip from the remote area where we lived to the city of Tamale' and to the airport to pick up mission teams. We purchased necessary supplies and always stopped by the bank to exchange money.

As the van pulled into the bank parking lot, the Lord asked me to take 200 Ghana cedi's out of the bank, using my bankcard, and give two women one hundred Ghana cedi's each. I did as the Lord asked, of course; I withdrew money from the bank and put the money into my backpack. I returned to the van to wait for the missionaries to conclude their banking.

I sat in the front passenger seat for a while with the driver who worked for the mission. He was tall and thin and a Muslim. He was an excellent driver and knew every little village and goat trail for miles around. He drove miles and miles on difficult, dusty, dirt roads to dozens of remote villages. He was great at taking care of flat tires and minor engine problems.

The air conditioner did not work in the van and it was a blistering hot day. I decided to stand in the shade. As I got out of the van, I left my backpack behind. I was away for only a short time before I remembered and returned to get it. I immediately checked to make sure the money was there. It was gone. The van was never out of my sight and no one had entered or left during the time I had stepped away. I knew the driver had stolen the money. I could tell by the way that he was acting that he knew that I knew he had stolen the money.

I was offended and became angry. He deserved to be punished! At that moment, he was not worthy of love and respect. Deep down I wanted him to be punished. I was filled with fear and anxiety.

I took a moment to breathe and realized I had a real dilemma. Even though he had been driving for the ministry for some time, and had heard teaching about Jesus, he was a Muslim. Many people in Ghana are very poor and believe that stealing is okay. Although I had not known him long, I had been doing my best to treat him with respect and develop a good relationship with him. I wanted to let my light shine and hoped that he would see Christ in me. What should I do? I could accuse him and tell him to give the money back. If he refused, I could ask someone to search him. I suppose I could even call the police and have him arrested. Would he lose his job? What about his family? I was not sure how to handle this.

I began to think about the grace that Jesus has showered on me. If I do not respond in love, then I am belittling what Jesus did on the cross. He died so that I might walk in forgiveness and be in right relationship with him and with others. Jesus has forgiven my sin countless times. Shouldn't I be willing to forgive the driver? I am not saying that people should always be given a "Get Out of Jail Free" card. It is just that Jesus took the punishment for me so before I pass judgment, wouldn't it be wise to think about handling the situation in a way that Jesus might handle it? (1 John 4:11) If I do not try, then how can I make a difference? This scripture came to mind.

> *You are the __salt__ of the earth; but if the salt loses its flavor, how shall it be seasoned? It is then good for nothing but to be thrown out and trampled underfoot by men. You are the __light__ of the world. A city that is set on a hill cannot be hidden. Nor do they light a lamp and put it under a basket, but put it on a lampstand, and it gives light to all who are in the house. Let your light so shine before men, that they may see your good works and glorify your Father in heaven.*
> *—Matthew 5:13-16 (emphasis mine)*

<u>Salt</u> preserves and <u>light</u> shines. At the time that Matthew wrote this, salt was used to preserve food. Light was used to shine into the darkness. If I am the salt of the earth, doesn't that mean that I should preserve people? If I am the light of the world, shouldn't I light the way for others?

I took a deep breath and prayed silently until some of the emotion subsided and my tensed muscles began to relax. "Lord, forgive me for letting my emotions get the better of me. Please tell me what to do."

I was filled with love and heard that still small voice: "Do nothing."

"All right, Lord," I replied.

I still had a dilemma, however. The Lord had asked me to get the money from the bank for the two women I would see tomorrow. Now I did not have the money. I had withdrawn all of the money that I had. I only had $300 in the bank when I got on the plane to be a missionary in Ghana. I felt like I was letting the Lord down. I felt sick about this as I rode back to the mission house with the missionaries.

That night, I prayed, "Lord, forgive me for not being a good steward of the money as I should have been. I was careless. Please provide the money so I can give it away as you instructed."

I went to church the next morning and a missionary that I worked with walked over to me before the service began. He said, "The Lord told me that it is important that I give you two hundred Ghana cedi's this morning. He didn't say why you needed this money, but here it is." He handed me the cedi's.

I laughed and said, "You have no idea how much I needed this money. I asked the Lord to provide and now He has! Thank you for giving me the money. Thank you for helping me be obedient."

After the church service, I gave the money to the two young women as the Lord had instructed. They were overwhelmed. One of the women said, "I prayed and asked the Lord for money to pay for my school fees. He has answered my prayer!" She was giddy with excitement.

The other young woman was so surprised that she had difficulty finding the right words to say. Her eyes welled up with tears and she hugged me. This was not a typical thing for her to do. She pulled me aside later and thanked me saying, "I am sorry I did not know what to say when you gave the money to me. I thank the Lord for you and for the money. By God's grace, I knew He would provide."

I was thankful I had listened to the Lord and remained silent about the theft. As I had mentioned, the Muslim man who had stolen the money from me was a good driver. I spent a lot of time riding on those bumpy, broken roads with him. He would not make eye contact with me at first. Shame always makes us hide. I was not going to let what he did influence our relationship. I prayed, "Lord, show me how to love him. Let him see You in me."

I talked with him about his family and about the Muslim faith. I shared American peanut butter and granola bars from my care packages with him. I treated him to minerals (soft drinks) on dry, hot days. Little by little, I saw a change in him. Pretty soon, instead of sleeping in the vehicle while we were working in the villages, he was there sitting with the people listening to me teach and tell stories of what the Lord had done in my life. A smile would fill his face when he saw me.

Sin never hides for long, however. Sometimes the truth comes out in embarrassing ways. The driver was eventually caught stealing again and was publically humiliated.

I went home and prayed, "Lord, my heart breaks for this man. What can I do to show him grace instead of condemnation?"

The Lord said, "Give him your pocket knife."

When packing for my trip I asked the Lord to show me what to take to such a remote place. Following God's instruction, I took tools, batteries, flashlights, and a multiple tool pocketknife in a leather case. I was thankful to have them.

I carried the knife with me each day as I prayed, "Lord, arrange the right time for me to talk with the driver. Help me know what to say."

When I saw him later, I asked my friend to translate for me because I wanted to make sure that he understood what I was saying to him. He had reverted to the old, shame-filled, staring down at the floor behavior. He did not want to look at me. I made him look me in the eyes and I said, "I forgive you for stealing money from me several months ago."

He grinned a sheepish grin of acknowledgement.

I waited until his gaze caught mine again and continued, "I want you to know that I love you and Jesus loves you. The Lord has forgiven me for my sin over and over again when I did not deserve it. It is because of His grace that I can forgive you."

He blinked his eyes at me, trying to take in what I was saying. He nodded his head.

I said, "I'd like to give you a gift."

I turned and pulled the pocketknife in the leather case out of my backpack and placed it into his hands. He was overwhelmed. His eyes widened and that familiar grin filled his face again.

"Now you won't have to strip anymore wires using your teeth," I giggled.

He was at a loss for words. He laughed and kept saying my name over and over and over. "Misty, Misty, Misty, Misty!" Then he surprised me by reaching out and giving me a quick hug, something he had never done before.

I do not know if he ever accepted Jesus. As a Muslim, if he turned his back on his faith, his family would disown him and he would lose everything that he had. I trust the Lord is working in his life and pray he will one day see the light.

Living under the law and living with offense separates us from others. It makes us guarded and overwhelms us with emotions. It clouds our ability to hear from God and we often make decisions based on emotion. This hinders our walk of faith.

"Grace has to be the loveliest word in the English language. It embodies almost every attractive quality we hope to find in others. Grace is a gift of the humble to the humiliated. Grace acknowledges the ugliness of sin by choosing to see beyond it. Grace accepts a person as someone worthy of kindness despite whatever grime or hard-shell casing keeps him or her separated from the rest of the world. Grace is a gift of tender mercy when it makes the least sense."

—Charles R. Swindoll

Chapter Five

SOUL FOOD, CAR KEYS AND LIVING WATER

"Tomorrow, and tomorrow, and tomorrow, creeps in this petty pace from day to day to the last syllable of recorded time...."
—"Macbeth," Act 5, Scene 5, William Shakespeare

I t is easy to spend all of our time and energy focusing on what we do day-to-day and on where we are going. It is far better, however, to focus on who we are becoming. If we become the people God created us to be, we will make the most out of our day-to-day and even glorify God through it all.

I was going through a very difficult time in my life. Even though I am never separated from God, I felt very far away from Him. I felt tiny, like a small child toddling alone down a desolate road. I was empty, discouraged, and frustrated. I slipped into a little blue funk. On the inside, I was as dry as overcooked toast! My flesh was feeling a little cumbersome. I read the Bible, but the words dissolved into the page. I could not comprehend what I was reading. I began to cry out to the Lord for comfort, wisdom, guidance and encouragement. Then something amazing happened!

I went to visit Helen one Saturday morning. Although she did not know that I was coming, she was not surprised to see me. Smiling, she invited me in and said, "I am glad you are here. The Lord told me you were coming today."

Helen took my hand and led me over to a table in the room. The table was full of journals, Bibles and devotion books, all opened to certain pages. She handed me a pen and an empty notebook, then waved her hand over the table and said, "Feast."

As I poured over the journal pages and scripture, I began to weep. Everything that I was reading was exactly what I needed. The words were water for a thirsty soul. I had not told anyone what was in my heart. Yet everything was there on the pages. Only the Lord knew. Helen simply opened the journals, devotion books and Bibles to the pages as the Lord directed. She listened to His instructions and prepared a table laden with soul food for me.

"God uses broken things. It takes broken soil to produce a crop, broken clouds to give rain, broken grain to give bread, broken bread to give strength. It is the broken alabaster box that gives forth perfume. It is Peter, weeping bitterly, who returns to greater power than ever."

—Vance Havner

Helen documented her life by writing in a journal each day during Bible study and quiet time. She had over three hundred green, hardback, lined accounting-style journals in her closet. I spent most of the day pouring over everything, crying and talking with Jesus. I left there feeling loved, encouraged, and with a focused determination about my life.

I began having a regular quiet time and Bible study each day, but still I struggled. My mind wandered or I gave in to interruptions. I even fell asleep. I was discouraged and talked with Helen, "Do you ever have trouble when you are having your quiet times with the Lord? To be honest, I struggle sometimes."

She smiled and said, "A couple doesn't set an alarm to make love."

I was shocked! I was not expecting that. My facial expression must have given me away. Helen let the moment linger for a while and said, "Misty, you just do not know how much the Lord loves you. Sometimes that love moves us toward obedience." It would be years later before I would fully understand and experience this for myself.

Helen had a car that she had driven for years. Once dependable, now it would not run properly. She put her case before the Lord and prayed, "Lord, I thank you for providing my car. It has been faithful for many years, but Lord, now I need a new one. You are my provider and I can count on you. I believe it by faith. Thank you, Lord! In Jesus' Name, amen."

I asked, "Ms. Helen, did you try to find a car?"

She said, "No, the Lord didn't tell me to do anything, so I waited."

I asked, "Did you call anyone or talk to anyone about it?"

Helen replied, "No. Once I gave it to the Lord, it was done. I believe it by faith. If He directed me to do something then I would do what He asked, but He didn't. He promised He would provide as He has always done. I believed Him."

There was no wavering of her faith. It never crossed her mind that the prayer would not be answered. I went to visit a couple of weeks later and noticed a new car sitting by the curb. I said, "Helen, tell me about the car."

She said, "Oh, isn't it nice? A doctor came by and told me that He wanted to go and get a different car and the Lord told him to give that one to me." She pointed at the car while looking out of the window. "He just came to my apartment and gave me the keys and the paperwork. It's all mine and it is perfect for me! Praise the Lord! He has even paid the fees and insurance." Providing a new car is a small thing to God. Helen took the Word of God to heart!

When we have divine encounters, it proves the will of God.

Therefore, I urge you, brothers and sisters, in view of God's mercy, to offer your bodies as a living sacrifice, holy and pleasing to God—this is your true and proper worship. Do not conform to the pattern of this world, but be transformed by

the renewing of your mind. Then you will be able to test and approve what God's will is—his good, pleasing and perfect will.
　　　　　　　　　　　　　—Romans 12:1-2 (emphasis mine)

A renewed mind is not simply being able to quote scripture or having a Biblical answer for a problem. Encounters with Jesus, like receiving a car or vegetable soup, transform the way we think. These kinds of encounters change our convictions. The renewed mind proves the will of God and allows us to witness the evidence of God on earth. We can, through the way God moves in our lives, prove that He is authentic!

Why would the Lord want us to give approval for His will? We are the body and He is the head. He is looking for a body that will fully co-operate with the head.

And he is the head of the body, the church; he is the beginning and the firstborn from among the dead, so that in everything he might have the supremacy.
　　　　　　　　　　　　　—Colossians 1:18 (emphasis mine)

When we are born again, we (His body) are empowered to do the same things that Jesus did (John 14:12). As we grow in our relationship with Jesus, we learn to walk in the authority given to us. We expect to have one glorious experience after another.

"If you are renewed by grace, and were to meet your old self, I am sure you would be very anxious to get out of his company."
　　　　　　　　　　　　　—Charles H. Spurgeon

Sin can make us impotent. All have sinned and fallen short of the glory of God. How can there be honor and glory when we are impotent?

This righteousness from God comes through faith in Jesus Christ to all who believe. There is no difference, for all have sinned

and fall short of the glory of God, and all are justified freely
by his grace through the redemption that came by Christ Jesus.
God presented Christ as a sacrifice of atonement, through the
shedding of his blood—to be received by faith.
—Romans 3:22-25 (emphasis mine)

We do not have to live an impotent life. Jesus said that if we believe in him we would have <u>rivers of living water</u> flowing out of us.

On the last day, that great day of the feast, Jesus stood and
cried out, saying, "If anyone thirsts, let him come to Me and
drink. He who believes in Me, as the Scripture has said, out
of his heart will flow <u>rivers of living water</u>." But this He spoke
concerning the Spirit, whom those believing in Him would
receive; for the Holy Spirit was not yet given, because Jesus
was not yet glorified.
—John 7:37-39, NKJV (emphasis mine)

Jesus is talking about the <u>Holy Spirit</u> that now lives within each Christian. If our hearts are right, we have everything we need to do what is required in life, even the most unexpected things.

This is a recollection from my African journal. A steady stream of people walked down the road carrying bowls and bags of cassava, groundnuts, millet and other goods to sell. They would stop by the mission and greet us, then leave their cell phones to charge while they went to market. There was no electricity in their villages. The mission office was there at the Baptist Church.

Many of the local tribes in the area worshiped evil spirits as a part of the African traditional religion. There are no church buildings or temples but the fetish priests use fear to manipulate, demanding blood sacrifices in exchange for the favor of the evil spirits. It is all the work of Satan and is very real, very dark and very evil. Dealing with curses, evil spirits, Ju Ju, sickness and disease, and every other work of the devil was a daily reality. Some days we would feel so oppressed that we would spend the first few hours of the day in prayer until the oppression lifted. We prayed so we could breathe again.

Many people came to the mission on market day and asked for us to pray with them. They endured incredible hardship, poverty and living conditions. These villagers depended upon the Lord for survival. I was in the church praying with several of our pastors when the Lord spoke to me, "That woman is in pain. If you pray with her, I will heal her."

A woman from one of the villages had come with her pastor. She did not ask for prayer but she was sitting in a chair, head bowed, silently praying. Gladys, one of our staff members, translated for me and I asked the woman, "Are you in pain?"

She said, "Yes, I am in terrible pain all over. It hurts to move at all. I have been in pain for a long time, but by God's grace I believe I will be healed." She winced in pain simply lifting her head to talk with me.

I smiled and encouraged her, "The Lord told me that you are in pain, but He is going to heal you. May I pray for you?"

She smiled and nodded, "Yes, please."

We anointed her with oil, gently laid our hands on her and prayed for healing. She began feeling better immediately. She thanked us and then went on her way to market. We saw her later that afternoon and she was rejoicing! Her pain was gone. She had been completely healed! The woman was persistent in prayer and expected to be healed.

It is fun when the Lord tells us ahead of time that He is going to heal someone. I cannot think of a better way to show the love of Christ. I am thankful I was obedient and stepped out in faith. I am thankful for the Holy Spirit.

"It may be hard for an egg to turn into a bird: it would be a jolly sight harder for it to learn to fly while remaining an egg. We are like eggs at present. And you cannot go on indefinitely being just an ordinary, decent egg. We must be hatched or go bad."

—C. S. Lewis

Chapter Six

MOBILE HOMES, A HARPIST, AND RAMEN NOODLES

"If it suddenly became impossible for us to cover up all the junk we normally hide from the rest of humanity, I have a feeling we would all get real motivated to deal with the source of what ails us."

—Andy Stanley,
*It Came from Within: The Shocking Truth
of What Lurks in the Heart*

And the Lord God formed man of the dust of the ground, and breathed into his nostrils the breath of life; and man became a <u>living being</u>.

—Genesis 2:7 (emphasis mine)

H<u>uman beings</u> are intricately designed and amazing. There is actually more to us than meets the eye.

Now may the God of Peace Himself sanctify you completely; and may your whole <u>spirit, soul and body</u> be preserved blameless at the coming of our Lord Jesus Christ.

—1 Thessalonians 5:23 (emphasis mine)

Human beings are made up of three parts: the <u>body, the soul and the spirit.</u> Our body is aware of the world and of the way the world works. Our soul is consumed with things related to our desires and emotions. Our spirit is aware of and communicates with God. If we walk into a room and feel the presence of God, our spirit enables us to have that experience. Let's look at this more closely.

First, the <u>body</u> is the fleshly, mobile home in which we live and walk around. Our bodies are affected by the decisions that we make. Our bodies can be injured, and acquire sickness or diseases. Our bodies change all of the time. We will eventually die and be eaten by worms. Yuck! Our physical bodies respond to many things.

When the temperature changes from hot to cold, we begin to shiver.

When a ball is thrown at our faces, we put our hands up to protect ourselves.

When we hear something scary, it gives us goose bumps.

We smell apple pie cooking and our mouths water.

A man sees a beautiful woman and there is a physical response.

A hiker stumbles and quick reflexes keep him from falling on his face.

In an emergency our body responds so well, it goes into something called "fight or flight."

We have all heard stories of heroism. A driver does not notice the little girl behind him, backs the car up and hears a thump. A panic stricken mother lifts the car off her daughter. It should have been physically impossible for the mother to pick up that car, but she did it.

Fight or flight happens during emergencies or traumatic experiences. Our bodies automatically compensate so we can handle the situation.

The stomach stops digesting its food.

The mouth dries up.

The muscles tighten.

The heart pumps more blood.

The senses are heightened.

Adrenaline shoots into the bloodstream.

The cortisol levels increase.

We began to burn fuel and start sweating.

Amazing, isn't it? After the crisis is over, our bodies should calm down, began to function normally and return to a more peaceful state.

If we are full of fear and anxiety, however, our bodies still respond as though we are in a "fight or flight" mode. Our bodies remain in high gear. It is a like a car parked with the engine running. The driver presses his foot down hard on the accelerator. More acceleration places more stress on the engine. The car is not designed to run that way; our bodies are not either. If we are always stressed, anxiety ridden and full of fear, our physical bodies will be affected and eventually we will become sick. So how do we live a life that is not in high gear?

We have been given everything that we need to live a Godly life. We are alive in Christ Jesus. We have a desire to put others first. We must learn to appropriate what is ours through the Holy Spirit and the Word of God. If we are sensitive and led by the Spirit, we will not fulfill the sinful desires of the flesh (2 Peter 1:3-4).

There is a struggle in everyone. Even the most sincere Christians struggle. Think about it. You go to a restaurant to eat. You are hungry, so you order an appetizer. Then the waiter brings the bread with butter. Everything looks and smells so good that you devour the food. Then the meal comes and you eat all of it. Yum! Your pants are too tight, so you loosen your belt. You are having a little trouble breathing because your lungs are squished up under your rib cage. You secretly wish you were wearing sweat pants. The waiter comes to your table and says, "Would you like to see the dessert menu?" You think, *Why not?*

You look at the person with you and say, "Let's split a dessert. Why not live a little?" Then you leave, feeling miserable. Honest confession is good for the soul, right? I have done this and on more than one occasion. Where should we draw the line concerning gluttony? I do not know, but I am sure it was crossed.

"My doctor told me to stop having intimate dinners for four. Unless there are three other people."
—Orson Welles

The flesh wants to suppress or influence the Spirit and the Spirit wants to suppress or influence the flesh. I watched a cartoon when I was a little girl. It showed a man with an angel holding a harp standing on one shoulder, and a devil holding a pitchfork standing on the other shoulder. The angel tried to talk the man into doing the right thing. The devil tried to talk the man into doing the wrong thing. The cartoon could have gone something like this.

The man finds a wallet that someone had accidentally dropped. It is full of money. The devil says, "Wow, look at all that money. It's all yours."

The angel says, "See that man over there? He is the one who dropped it. You should return it to him."

The devil: "Don't listen to that harpist. That guy won't even miss it."

The angel: "Returning that man's wallet is the right thing to do."

The devil says, "Now you can buy that new television that you have been saving for. Go to the store now."

Invariably, the man made the wrong choice and always got into some kind of hilarious trouble. Learning through cartoons was fun! We do feel like that man sometimes, don't we?

When we have these temptations or feelings and desires, we think something must be wrong with us. We must be the only person who is struggling. We try to hide it. Then we usually come up with a list of rules. We think, *If I can just follow a set of rules, it will make things right*. We fall into legalism. We are unable to keep the rules so we began to grade ourselves. *I messed up this week, about a "D" effort. I'll try harder next week. Maybe I'll get a "B"*. Pretty soon we become so frustrated that we throw our hands up and say, "Enough of this!" and walk away. Sometimes we will even try to blame things on someone else. <u>Blame</u> started in the garden. It was <u>the woman's</u> <u>fault</u> after all! Adam said so!

> *Then the man (Adam) said, "<u>The woman whom You gave to be</u>*
> *<u>with me</u>, <u>she gave me</u> of the tree, and I ate."*
> *—Genesis 3:12 (emphasis mine)*

The Bible does not say, "If I don't fulfill the lusts of the flesh then I can walk in the spirit." No!

> *I say then: <u>Walk in the Spirit</u>, and <u>you shall not fulfill the lust</u>*
> *<u>of the flesh</u>. For the flesh lusts against the Spirit, and the Spirit*

*against the flesh and these are contrary to one another, so that
you do not do the things that you wish.*
                              —Galatians 5:16 (emphasis mine)

Paul in Galatians is saying that if we live by the spirit then we will
not fulfill the desires of a sinful nature. The Holy Spirit has broken the
power of the flesh; but the flesh is never satisfied, so we must crucify it.
The flesh cannot be reformed or rehabilitated. We cannot negotiate with
it. We must consider it dead even though it is still kicking. We are born
by the Spirit, given gifts by the Spirit, and operate in the Spirit. We are
in process. The Holy Spirit will help produce the character of Christ in
us. If we are walking in the Spirit, we will produce fruit. Fruit cannot
be created in a factory with sweat and works. Fruit is picked fresh. The
best fruit is usually attached to the <u>vine</u> or fed straight from the root.

*Jesus said, "<u>I am the vine</u>, you are the branches. He who abides
in Me, and I in him, bears much fruit; for without Me you can
do nothing."*
                              —John 15:5 (emphasis mine)

The second part of our make-up is the <u>soul, which is our mind,
our will and our emotions.</u> Our mind is our thinker. It is the part of
us that reasons, retains information, and makes decisions. Much of
our lives are determined by what we believe and the choices that we
make. Our memories are stored in our minds. Our brains can recall
any experience. We have the amazing ability of processing things in
an instant. We respond or react to those things that we think about,
sometimes involuntarily.

A mom and her six-year-old son approached me one day at church.
She said, "He has something that he wants to tell you."

I knelt down so I could be on his level and look him straight in the
eyes. In his most grown up voice and with a serious face he said, "Ms.
Misty, I have a problem."

I asked, "What is it?"

He said, "There is this little wax bug that crawls up inside of my
ear." He illustrates by pointing into his ear. "It whispers to my brain
and makes me do things that I am not supposed to do!"

Out of the mouths of children! I bet most of us deep down wish that we could use that as an excuse for some of the lousy decisions we have made in our lives! What we believe about ourselves is important. If we believe we cannot do something or that we can do something, we are usually right! If we truly believe and open ourselves up to be used by God, we can change the world. If we don't, we won't.

Another part of our soul is our will. That is the part of us that determines what we will or will not do.

> *"I will eat a third piece of cake!"*
> *"I will not clean my room!"*
> *"No one is looking, I will take the money!"*

A married man thinks, "I will have only lunch with the beautiful lady I just met. There is nothing wrong with having lunch. Everyone has to eat, right?" That is how affairs begin. There is usually a long list of bad decisions made before we really get into trouble. Our will reinforces what we decide with our mind. When training, an athlete can take his body to the place of exhaustion because he believes that it is necessary. He wills himself to push past the pain his body is experiencing until he has accomplished his goals. The mind and the will work together. It can be for our good or to our detriment. Next to our salvation, free will is the greatest gift that has ever been given to us!

The Appalachian Trail is approximately 2,180 miles long and runs from Georgia to Maine. A couple of friends decided they wanted to start in Georgia and thru-hike the trail all the way to the end. It would take a year. They planned the trip for months, saving money, buying the best boots and gear and organizing food packages to be mailed all along the route. They started hiking and willed their way through bloody blisters, bruises, aches and pains. They endured rain, heat and the freezing cold. They slept on the ground, bathed in streams, and ate a lot of Ramen noodles. They had the greatest experience of their lives. It was the hardest, most unforgettable and rewarding thing they had ever done. They wanted to give up and quit on more than one occasion, but they made up their minds and willed their way forward. I admire their tenacity! They became part of a small minority of people who have hiked the entire Appalachian Trail. Makes us wonder if there is anything that we need to set our minds and <u>will</u> to do

<u>Our emotions are the third part of our soul</u>. Basically, those are our feelings of happiness, sadness, anger, joy, frustration, love, or fear. Everything stirs up our emotions. We hear a song on the radio and we immediately remember an old relationship that we once had and all of those old emotions come to the surface. We smell something and it reminds us of our grandmother, standing in the kitchen cooking as she always did. We can almost taste the cookies she used to bake. At once we are flooded with all those old feelings.

Emotions make everything feel very real. They make us feel alive. The way we respond to our emotions can either be a blessing to us or a hindrance to us. Satan uses fear and it can paralyze us. Jesus understands our emotions because He experienced them also. God is love and love is a very powerful emotion.

<u>The Lord communicates with us through our emotions</u>. For example, you are going about a normal day and for some reason you begin to think about someone. You cannot get her off your mind. You do not know why, you just do. Inside you feel as though something is wrong. So you take a moment and pray that the Lord will help that person and give her peace. Why do you pray that? You pray what you feel about her on the inside. The first chance you have, you pick up the phone and call her. She tells you that she just lost her job. She is afraid. She asks, "How did you know something was wrong? I cannot tell you how much it means to me that you called me. Thank you!" You are obedient to God's will and set yourself up to be used by Him.

<u>The final part of our make-up is our spirit.</u> Here we find our <u>character, nature and personality</u>. Our <u>character</u> is who we are; much of our mental and moral qualities are learned. Good character traits are honesty, integrity, sincerity, generosity, goodness, or self-control. For those with bad character, the opposite is true.

Then there is our <u>nature</u>, which is our disposition or temperament. I know some people who are so laid back that nothing ever seems to bother or frustrate them. Others are nervous and tightly wound.

Our <u>personalities</u> demonstrate our emotions and our behavioral tendencies. We often say that a person is outgoing, never meets a stranger, and loves to be the center of attention. Some we describe as introverted or wallflowers. We want to spend time with some people because we like their personalities. It is important that we understand our make-up, because it is a part of how the Lord communicates to us through the Holy Spirit. The Holy Spirit works with our spirits, our minds and our emotions. God is love and love is a very powerful emotion. When we feel loved by God, we are using that loving part of our soul to communicate.

There is so much in the scripture that will help us if we will take advantage of it. This verse is key!

Love the Lord your God with all of your <u>heart</u> and with all your <u>soul</u> and with all your <u>strength</u> and with all your <u>mind</u>, and, <u>love your neighbor as yourself</u>."

—Luke 10:27, NIV (emphasis mine)

God did not intend for us to separate ourselves from <u>His presence</u>, from <u>other people</u>, or be separated <u>within ourselves</u>.

When we become angry with God because He did not do something we wanted Him to do, <u>we put up a big wall and separate ourselves from Him</u>. We may even become angry if we see God blessing someone else and answering the prayers of others. We are envious. We are unable to celebrate the blessings of others.

We usually respond in one of two ways. First, we might become insecure, acquire a defeatist attitude and begin to believe that God must not love us. *Why would God want to answer my little prayer, anyway?* We feel sorry for ourselves and turn our backs on Him. Secondly, we can become so bitter that we respond with pride and arrogance. We behave as if we have all of the answers and actually know more than God. We push back against Him and against anyone else who might tell us the truth. Pride rarely recognizes itself in the mirror. It is very noticeable for everyone else, however. We chain ourselves to a wall of separation that is of our own making. God understands what we are going through, yet He never, ever separates Himself from us.

I talked with a man who was so angry that he turned his back on God and walked away from his faith. He had prayed and asked for a promotion in his job. He worked long hours and did everything his bosses asked him to do, but they gave the promotion to someone else.

It is tough when we pray and the answer is "no" and we do not know why. This is where our faith is tested. Do we trust that God is on our side even when He does not give us what we have asked for? Do we believe that God has a better plan? I do not know why my grandmother died at the beginning of her retirement. She missed the best time of her life. I do not know why my friend's apartment burned down. She lost everything that she owned! We may never know why these things happen, but the way we handle these situations places our character under a magnifying glass. It says a lot about our faith.

The man who lost the promotion was furious. Instead of talking with his bosses about their decision, he became difficult and prideful. Instead of going to God for help, he turned his back on Him. The man was eventually fired, losing everything that he had worked so hard to achieve. He eventually regretted his behavior. It took years for him to find his way back to his faith.

Sometimes we have disagreements with people. We become hurt or angry and we separate ourselves from others. We even say things such as, "I hope I never see him again," or, "I will never speak to her again for as long as I live." We do our best to avoid or ignore the person. In separating ourselves from people with an unforgiving spirit, we separate ourselves from God.

When my nephew Jordan was a little boy, if he encountered something that he did not like he said, "I can't like that!" It has become a family joke, but there is truth in it.

Our identity or the way in which we see ourselves is also very important. If we do not feel loved, necessary, needed or included, then this will eventually affect our self-image. We will feel sorry and belittle ourselves. Sometimes we set unrealistic goals and feel like a failure when we do not meet those goals. Sometimes we feel condemned when we do not meet the expectations of other people. All of these things will greatly affect us in a negative way. We must believe that God created us in His image and loves us just as we are.

For you created my inmost being; you knit me together in my mother's womb. I praise You because I am fearfully and wonderfully made; Your works are wonderful, I know that full well. My frame was not hidden from You when I was made in the secret place, when I was woven together in the depths of the earth. Your eyes saw my unformed

71

body; all the days ordained for me were written in your book before one of them came to be.
—Psalm 139:13-16 (emphasis mine)

When we live under self-condemnation and do not see ourselves as God sees us, God is heartbroken. A <u>separation</u> of sorts happens on the inside of us. Separation of any kind can cause us to be sick. Loving, even loving ourselves, is easier said than done. We understand the importance of loving God. We ask God to help us love others, especially those who are difficult to love. Sometimes when we make mistakes, we judge ourselves harshly. We will often take responsibility for things for which we are not responsible. We pick up burdens the Lord never intended for us to carry. We ask God to forgive us. We forgive others. We have the hardest time forgiving ourselves.

Let me share a story with you that illustrates how important our bodies, souls, and spirits are and how they work together. I met Jeanine on a Friday evening. She had been suffering from rheumatoid arthritis, an illness that causes painful inflammation and stiffness of the joints. She had been to every doctor, taken every medicine and had every treatment. Nothing worked. She was at a place of desperation. The arthritis was so painful she could barely walk. Jeanine is a Christian and loves the Lord. She had studied the Bible and understood it. She believed in healing and had asked the Lord for it, but was still suffering. She was willing to do whatever it took to receive healing. I helped her carefully, painfully walk into the house so I could take her through a healing prayer.

A merry heart does good, like medicine, but <u>a broken spirit dries the bones</u>.
—Proverbs 17:22, NKJV (emphasis mine)

I asked, "Jeanine, what has happened in your life that caused you to feel <u>broken</u> on the inside?" I knew Jeanine had a <u>broken spirit</u>.

Without hesitation she said, "Thirteen years ago my husband committed suicide. He had suffered with depression for a long time."

I asked, "When did you begin to have arthritis?"

She paused a moment as she thought about it and said, "Come to think of it, it was about thirteen years ago."

We talked for a while about her life prior to her husband's suicide. Her life was filled with responsibilities of rearing the children, running their business, taking everyone to church, making sure that everything and everyone was taken care of. She knew that her husband needed help and found a counselor for him. Even though she had done everything humanly possible to help him, she carried the guilt and shame of his death. She picked up that burden and condemned herself. Where in the Word of God does it say we are responsible for someone else's choices? Nowhere!

We cripple ourselves with the "would have, should have, could have" questions. "I wish I could have done this," or, "I should have done that." Bad experiences from the past cannot be changed and it is unhealthy to bring those things into the present. Jeanine was broken on the inside and her body responded. It turned on itself. That is what a broken spirit does. Our bodies will come into agreement with what our minds tell us. If we tell ourselves we are worthless, then we will begin to believe the lie and our bodies will respond. She stopped loving herself, she felt condemned, unworthy, and full of shame. None of those things are from God.

As we talked, Jeanine began to realize that her thinking did not line up with the Word of God. As her mind shifted to the correct way of thinking, a righteous indignation rose up within her.

She said, "I am not responsible for what he did! I did everything that I could! I refuse to carry that responsibility anymore!"

I said, "That's right! Now let's give these things to the Lord. He suffered and died for us so we wouldn't have to carry these burdens."

We prayed and asked the Lord to forgive her for taking the responsibility for her husband's death. She realized she should have turned everything over to the Lord. We prayed specifically and asked the Lord to forgive her for every burden she carried.

We had not even prayed for healing when Jeanine said, "My feet aren't hurting anymore."

We did not stop there. We prayed for a while longer. On the following Sunday morning, my sister Stormy saw Jeanine in church. She was ecstatic! She got up danced and wiggled her feet and joints around to show Stormy that she had been completely and totally healed! Jeanine had lined up her life with the Word of God. She took the truth of the Word and with her mind believed. She exercised her free will, prayed out loud and surrendered everything to Jesus. Her body responded by going back into divine alignment. Her body stopped turning on itself. That was over ten years ago and Jeanine is still healed. A grateful Jeanine goes hiking as a way of celebration. She said, "I will never take the ability to walk for granted again!" Praise God!

It is important that we understand how God created us. Our being should live and move with the Holy Spirit. When we separate ourselves from God or others, we take love out of the picture. When we walk in condemnation, it makes forgiveness difficult. We remove the possibility of reconciliation, healing, and unity. Love is a most powerful thing. Love comes from God because God is love and we are created in His image. Love has the power to change everything!

"From the heart arise unknowable impulses as well as conscious feelings, moods, and wishes. The heart, too, has its reasons and is the center of perception and understanding. Finally, the heart is the seat of the will: it makes plans and comes to good decisions. Thus the heart is the central and unifying organ of our personal life. Our heart determines our personality, and is therefore not only the place where God dwells but also the place to which Satan directs his fiercest attacks. It is this heart that is the place of prayer. The prayer of the heart is a prayer that directs itself to God from the center of the person and thus affects the whole of our humanness."

—Henri J.M. Nouwen,
The Way of the Heart: Desert Spirituality and Contemporary Ministry

---

Chapter Seven

A Grouch, Emails and a Jilted Bride

"Love can change a person the way a parent can change a baby-awkwardly, and often with a great deal of mess."
—Lemony Snicket, *Horseradish*

Love is crazy, unpredictable, and intangible. When we fall in love, reason and common sense sometimes go right out the window. We find ourselves saying and doing things, for the sake of love, that we have never done before. We may even become reckless and make poor decisions. Our friends notice and immediately try measure what we are feeling, "How much do you love Him?" Can that question really be answered?

If we feel the need to measure our affection for Jesus, we have not truly experienced Him. If we have recklessly abandoned our lives to Jesus, our passion should defy reason. Passion comes from determined obedience. Recklessness for Jesus is not something that can be measured and it is not irrational or irresponsible, although our friends and family may disagree. This kind of passion will not make sense to people. The enemy will test our love for Jesus by offering excuses and distractions. We shortchange ourselves if we give in.

I know a pastor who was called to start a church. He was excited about it until God told Him to sell the house he had purchased for his wife and donate the money as a seed for the ministry. His wife loved that house. It was a difficult thing to do, but he did just that. They now have an even nicer home and His ministry has reached thousands. God always confirms reckless responsibility. If we are passionately committed to Jesus, He will move us beyond average living.

God has given us everything that we need to live a reckless, irrational life. When we are born again, God pours His love into our hearts and spirits through the Holy Spirit.

> *And hope does not put us to shame, because God's love has been poured out into our hearts through the Holy Spirit, who has been given to us.*
> *—Romans 5:5 (emphasis mine)*

In order to live a reckless life of unconditional love and obedience, we must sacrifice our selfishness. Once we receive the Holy Spirit and God's love is poured into our hearts, we become the loving people Paul talks about in 1 Corinthians. Love will pour from us as God's love was poured into us.

> *Dear friends, let us love one another, for love comes from God. Everyone who loves has been born of God and knows God. Whoever does not love does not know God, because God is love. This is how God showed his love among us: He sent his one and only Son into the world that we might live through him. This is love: not that we loved God, but that he loved us and sent his Son as an atoning sacrifice for our sins. Dear friends, since God so loved us, we also ought to love one another. No one has ever seen God; but if we love one another, God lives in us and his love is made complete in us.*
> *—1 John 4:8-12 (emphasis mine)*

> *Love is patient, love is kind. It does not envy, it does not boast, it is not proud. It does not dishonor others, it is not self-seeking,*

it is not easily angered, it keeps no record of wrongs. Love does not delight in evil but rejoices with the truth. It always protects, always trusts, always hopes, always perseveres. Love never fails… <u>It is the love of God Himself, who is love!</u>
—*1 Corinthians 13:4-8 (emphasis mine)*

To walk in love, the Spirit must dominate the flesh. <u>Love is patient, kind</u> and long suffering.

It is often difficult to be patient and kind. I began a job at a church and put together a team of volunteers to help in the ministry. I worked to know the people and helped them find a place where they could best serve. Organizing teams of people who were comfortable with each other was a challenge. Several people had warned me about one volunteer in particular.

I was told, "She is a grouch!"

One man said, "You will never be able to do anything right. She will criticize you no matter how well everything turns out."

Another lady said, "I would work in that ministry, but I cannot get along with that woman. She drives me crazy."

Someone else said, "If you kick that woman off the team, I'll come and help."

I always give people the benefit of the doubt, but it was not long before I found out that they were right. If I chose a certain song, she would suggest that another song would be better. If a team member had an idea, she would come up with five reasons that it would not work. I would think of the scripture: "Love is patient and kind." If we painted something green she would say it should have been red. I would think of the scripture: "Love does not keep a record of wrongs." A volunteer would step forward to teach a class and she would say, "*So and so would have done a much better job.*" I would think of the scripture: "Love is not easily provoked." This woman had the most critical spirit I had ever seen. My patience was wearing thin! She made everything difficult. I did not have much love in my heart for her.

I prayed, "Lord, please help me love her. My flesh wants to lash out at her. I know that she needs love. You say in the Word that we are not to be touchy or easily angered. I am struggling. Help me connect with her. Love her through me, please! Thanks, Lord. In Jesus' Name, amen."

I began to pray for her regularly. Every time I felt edgy or frustrated I would go back to the scripture (1 Corinthians 13). Soon the Lord put a love in my heart for her.

I asked her to come and work on a project with me. She was surprised. Most people had tiptoed around her. I knew that in working together I would have time alone with her. Before I could help her, I had to learn why she acted the way she did. As we worked together, I asked her to tell me about herself. If I knew her gifts, I could put her to work in an area in which she would shine. I discovered she was very creative. There was a big production coming up. I put her to work in an area where creativity was needed and gave her total control. She jumped at the chance. I worked along with her and complimented her. She did an excellent job and others recognized it.

We established an environment where no idea was a bad idea. Everyone began to share freely without the fear of being criticized. We began encouraging one another. The woman who had once been a pest, hindering everything, began to change. She became one of our most talented and dependable team members. People need to feel ownership in what they do. They want to be a part of something. They want to be loved and respected.

Our perceptions become our reality, even if what we perceive to be true isn't true. It is still true to us.

A friend talked with me one day. She said, "I have worked so hard to cultivate a friendship but my friend had to move away. I have e-mailed her at least a dozen times and she hasn't returned any of my e-mails. I am so upset that I have decided not to contact her anymore. If she wants to talk to me, she knows where to find me."

I asked, "Do you feel like your friend has rejected you?"

She said, "Yes!"

Now there was absolutely no evidence to substantiate that accusation. That was her perception; it was very real to her. I tried to help her look at things differently.

I asked her, "Is the friendship important to you?"

She said with a little pout, "Yes, and I thought it was important to her, too."

I said, "Moving to a new town, getting the house organized, and everything up and running can take some time. Not to mention starting the kids in a new school and getting used to a new job. If I were in your friend's shoes, I think I might need a little encouragement right now. How about continuing to send e-mails that contain prayers for her and scripture and words of encouragement? It might mean a lot to her."

That is what she did. She decided that she might have placed unrealistic expectations on her friend, so she changed the way she looked at everything. She took her eyes off of herself and began to find ways to love her friend.

After a couple of weeks, I got a phone call. She said, "I am so glad I contacted my friend. They had a lot of problems with the house when they got there and nothing has been working properly, including the Internet. She was thankful for the encouraging things I sent. She cried when she opened her e-mail. I am glad I was a good friend instead of the jerk that I might have been. I just wanted to say thanks for talking with me about everything."

God's love is a wonderful thing. Human love is selfish. The love of God through the Spirit is what empowers us. We must let the Holy Spirit within us dominate our flesh.

"I smooth her hair down over and over till she practically purring, feeling the love in my hand."
—Kathryn Stockett, *The Help*

I prayed for a lady who had been burdened for years by ungodly grief. She could not move past the loss and pain of a broken heart. She said, "I fell in love, had a wonderful courtship and got engaged. I was blessed with several bridal showers. I was so happy. On the day of the wedding, the church was beautifully decorated and everyone I loved was there. It was a perfect day, until my groom got cold feet and ran out of the church. I was embarrassed and crushed. He took the coward's way out and never talked with me about anything. I still do not know what went wrong! Not long after that I learned that he had married someone else."

She began to deeply grieve the loss. She was not able to move past the hurt and was stuck in the grief. She would not date anyone. She cried at the drop of a hat and began walling herself off from other people.

The Lord knows what we are going through. He does not want us lost in grief and living with someone else's decision. He wants us to move forward. Sorrow in itself does not produce anything but bad feelings. Grief hurts. It makes us either want to run and hide, as she was doing, or it makes us want to fight or strike back. Get revenge or retaliate!

When we are suffering from worldly grief we do not want to talk about it or face it. We will say, "Just drop it!" We may blame ourselves and become angry at our failure. Sometimes we become the center of attention. "Look at me. Can't you see that I am hurting? Come and take care of me."

Sometimes we blame others. All of these things lead to failure. We fall into bondage or into a prison of our own making. We justify our behavior. It produces resentment and bitterness that eats away at us. Each time we turn on ourselves our body follows. This leads to autoimmune diseases and infirmities.

Godly grief or sorrow leads us forward and to repentance. It acknowledges the truth and gets the thing that we need to deal with out into the open. Godly grief changes behavior and leads to freedom and deliverance. We will feel as though the monkey is off our backs and we enjoy things again. We must surrender everything to the Lord. We must let go of the hurt, anger, regret, lies, and fears and lay everything at His feet. We must ask Him to forgive us for taking those things upon ourselves. To repent means there has been a change of mind. We are turning away from our old way of doing things. We must ask the Lord to help us correct our thinking and move forward so we are not stuck living a half-life. We must crucify the flesh with our minds and hearts and come into agreement with the Word of God.

The jilted bride began to realize that she was feeling sorry for herself and that she was full of anger. She was not sleeping and did not feel well much of the time. Her stomach was in knots. She knew she had to change things. She put her cards on the table and she forgave the ex-groom. She stopped blaming herself for not being the perfect person. She began to see herself as Christ sees her. She completely changed her ungodly mindsets and shook off her worldly grief. She began feeling better almost immediately and was able to celebrate life and start dating again.

"Calvin: There's no problem so awful, that you can't add some guilt to it and make it even worse."
—Bill Watterson, *The Complete Calvin and Hobbes*

A Christian lady who was struggling with overcoming guilt came to me for prayer. She said, "I was pregnant and my husband and I were so excited. We began setting up a baby's nursery. We went to the doctor for a prenatal checkup, and they told me that the baby I was carrying was badly deformed and the brain was severely underdeveloped."

My heart broke for them. I said, "No!"

She nodded, "We didn't want to believe it so we went to more doctors and got several opinions. All of them urged us to terminate the pregnancy. We talked and prayed and weighed our options. It was agonizing! We eventually made the decision to do as the doctors had recommended. It was the most difficult thing I have ever had to go through."

Sympathizing with her I said, "I am so sorry."

She said, "To make matters worse, someone who was aware of the situation told me that I should not have aborted the baby because God could have healed that baby in my womb!" She was visibly upset and crying while telling me the story.

Why do some Christians feel the need to be critical of others? What happened to loving people through their pain? The hurtful comment made her feel worse. She was consumed with remorse, regret, guilt and shame.

Her mind was flooded with questions. She asked, "Is she right, could that baby have been healed or reformed in my womb? Did I do the right thing? Have I really messed up in God's eyes? Misty, I feel sick inside and there is no relief. Will I see my baby in heaven and will she know that I am her mother?"

Agony! She had been condemning herself for all of those years. I explained what the Bible says. We prayed and she forgave herself. She dealt with the grief and gave her burdens to the Lord. She left with a sense of peace.

I got a call a short time later. She said, "Today is the anniversary of the death of my baby. In the past I have spent the day in bed because I was in deep depression. It would have taken days to crawl out of it. Normally it is the worst day of my year. I wanted to let you know that I am different now. Today has been the best day! I have peace and I feel great! Thank you for praying with me."

Amazing things happen when we are obedient and line our lives with the Word of God. Miraculous things happen when we choose love, focus on our relationship with the Lord and really listen to Him. Love and acceptance are keys to walking in faith. If we do not believe God loves us, we will feel unworthy and never talk to Him. If we condemn ourselves we will feel God is condemning us and we will never talk to Him. If we feel we are not good enough we will feel He is judging us and not talk to Him. We certainly will never listen. We will never be obedient and we shortchange ourselves. We will miss a wonderful walk of faith and all of the blessings that come with it.

"All you need is love. But a little chocolate now and then doesn't hurt."

—Charles M. Schulz

Chapter Eight

A Lost Dog, a Waitress and a Patchwork Quilt

"We are all on a party line to God, but you, you setting right in his ear."

—Kathryn Stockett, *The Help*

It was easy for Helen to love people. I was amazed at how much Helen loved me. The Lord told Helen exactly what I needed. I had learned so much from her. One thing I did not completely understand, however, was how exactly to listen to the Lord when He spoke to me. Perhaps I lacked confidence or I was just being stubborn. Whatever the reasons, I knew I needed to understand how to hear the Lord. Helen could clearly hear everything the Lord told her. If she could hear and understand, so could I. So can you.

The first thing I learned was that the Lord wanted to talk to me, but I must take time to listen. If I ask Him a question, He really wants to answer. At that point, if I prayed at all it was a one-sided dialogue. It was all me. I was making suggestions to Him about what He should do to fix my problems. I was begging and pleading. Not very smart, huh? I think deep down I was afraid. I did not want to hear what the Lord might tell me. What if He asked me to do something that I did not want to do? What if it cost me something? What if God asked me to go somewhere I did not want to go? Perish the thought!

If I were honest with myself, there was an even deeper reason that I kept Him at a distance: I had heaped shovels of guilt upon myself because I did not think I was good enough. I was not even sure that God loved me. I was afraid He would point out my failures, faults and inadequacies. I did not want to think about that. Boy, not only was my cup half empty; it also had a leak in the bottom.

Then it dawned on me. I was making decisions based out of fear. It was upside down thinking. I began looking at what I believed and realized not one thing was based in scripture. God is love! He did not want to hurt me. That is not His character or His nature. I had studied enough of the Bible by that time to understand that. I was lost in ungodly mindsets. Now, instead of asking myself negative "what if" questions, I flipped it and asked positive "what if" questions.

What if there is something good in store for me?
What if the Lord wants to give me the desires of my heart?
What if He sends solutions to my problems?
What if He helps me financially?
What if He prospers me in my job?
What if I can live in good health?
What if He makes my home a happy place?

You get the idea. It took time and practice, but I learned. Pretty soon I was cheering on the inside. Go God! Wow. I was committed, no matter what.

What does the Lord sound like? I have had the most fun teaching children how to hear the Lord. When the Lord speaks to them and they understand, they show it in their little faces and in their body language. Many adults have been told that the Lord does not speak to people anymore and they believed it, so they stopped listening. Children have not been told that lie. Amazing things happen in the lives of those with childlike faith.

The Lord rarely speaks in an audible voice. The Lord does not sound like us. He does not say things in the way we might say them. It will not be like our personality. His voice will be different from who we are or how we say things. Have you ever said something that was so brilliant you thought, *I wonder where that came from?* That is because you were communicating something the Lord told you.

God communicates with us through the Holy Spirit. The Holy Spirit comes and lives inside of us, if we have asked Jesus into our hearts. His voice will not come from the outside as though we are listening to a stereo speaker. Instead, we will feel differently on the inside. I call it, "putting a knowing in your knower." I ask the children to think about what they feel like on the inside when they get a new puppy. How do they feel on Christmas morning? How do they feel when they spend time having fun with their best friends? The children will use words such as: happy, full, love, joy, fun, and excited. They can identify with those things.

That is what the Holy Spirit feels like. The Lord lets them know that He loves them through the Holy Spirit on the inside of them. At the same time He will speak to them or put a thought into their minds. I have found that the first thought is what the Lord tells us. The second thought is usually us talking ourselves out of what we have just heard.

In teaching the children to hear God's voice, I first ask them to close their eyes. I want them to focus on what the Lord is doing.

Second, I ask them to pray out loud by repeating after me, "Lord Jesus, please tell me that you love me." I watch them respond as they are filled to the brim with the love of God. Wonder fills them as they learn. Sometimes after that I ask, "Lord Jesus, please tell me one thing that you like about me." They then listen for the thought and pay attention to what they are feeling on the inside. The surprised expressions on their faces are wonderful! It is like asking Jesus to hug them. They feel so much love on the inside.

The third thing I ask the children to do is to repeat after me, "Lord Jesus, please tell me the name of someone that I could have been nicer to at school today?" Or perhaps, "What could I do to help Mom and Dad this week?" Sometimes I ask them questions that relate to what they are learning. They repeat it and then listen again. The expressions will change. I have them raise their hands when they have heard the Lord talk to them, then give them an opportunity to share what they have heard. Some of the things they have talked about have amazed me. Sometimes they will tell me in private because they do not want their friends to hear. It was between Jesus and them, anyway.

I always challenge them to do what they know they need to do even if it means changing some things. I hold them accountable, too. The next time I see them I ask what they did to make changes.

"Did you apologize to your friend after you hurt his feelings?"

"Did you clean up your room this week instead of hiding everything under your bed?"

"Did you study hard and ask the Lord to help you on your exam, or did you cheat again?"

After a while they come and tell me what the Lord told them. They share what the Lord is teaching them in their quiet time at home. They hear from the Lord and begin making wise decisions. Wow! It is actually like getting a phone call from a best friend. They do not need to ask who it is because they recognize their friend's voice. We recognize God's voice the same way we recognize the voice of our friends. The closer we grow in our relationship to Him, the more easily we will recognize His inner prompting in our spirits.

The Lord speaks to us in many ways. He communicates through the Word of God, through other people, and through circumstances. Many people who have difficulty hearing from God are usually not at peace on the inside. If we are anxious and feel a tornado on the inside, it is hard to discern the Lord's still small voice. We are not supposed to be anxious. If we forgive others and ourselves and if we turn all our cares over to Him, we should be at peace. If we are living in fear and not trusting the Lord, then anxiety will be our companion.

Let me share a story of someone who put what they had learned into practice. Jordan is a wonderfully gifted young girl who was in a children's Bible study class that I led on Sunday. Praying and listening to the Lord was a regular part of our mornings. We wrote our prayer requests on the board each week and then celebrated and talked about those prayers the Lord had answered in the previous week. We had experienced many miracles in that little class. Jordan was used to hearing from the Lord and to having prayers answered.

One night she and her family went out to dinner. When they returned home they discovered that someone had accidentally left the door open at her grandparents' house next door and their little dog had gotten out. The family decided to break up into groups and look for the dog in the neighborhood. Jordan had learned in our Bible study class that we should always turn to God first, following the prompting of the Holy Spirit, which is what she did.

She told her family that she believed if they prayed the Lord would bring the dog back. The family gathered together to pray. Jordan asked the Lord to keep the little dog safe and then thanked Him for bringing the dog home again. They went out and searched the neighborhood that night, but they did not find the dog.

I received a call from Courtney, Jordan's father, later that evening after they had looked for the dog and he told me what had happened. He was proud of Jordan because she had brought the family together to pray. He was also humbled by the faith of his little girl. He told me he had been having his own conversation with the Lord while standing outside on the deck that night. It went something like this: "Lord, losing a dog probably isn't a big deal in the scheme of things. I mean, if it were one of my children that was lost, that would be another story, I'd be praying like crazy! But Lord, it means a lot to my daughter Jordan and if you answer her prayer and bring the dog back safely, it will help solidify her faith in you. That would be wonderful." He thanked the Lord and turned everything over to Him. Then Courtney asked me if I would pray as well. I prayed with him over the phone and he agreed to keep me posted.

The next morning the veterinarian called. The dog had been dropped off at his office. You will love this! The lady who dropped the dog off gave us her side of the story. She was visiting from another state and staying at Laguna Beach Christian retreat near their house. She left her little dog at home and was missing him terribly. She was so used to sleeping with her dog that she had not had a good night's rest since she had been there. So as she walked on the beach she prayed and asked the Lord to send a little dog that would sleep on the bed with her.

When she got back to her room, the family's dog was sitting in front of her door. The neighbor said the dog had been staring at the door and occasionally barking for about an hour. There was no name or number on the collar. It was getting late, so she decided to take the dog inside. The dog curled up with her in the bed and made all of the sweet little dog noises that her dog made. For the first time since she had been there, she slept soundly through the night. The next morning she found the nearest veterinarian office, hoping they would recognize the little dog and contact the owners, which they promptly did.

The Lord answered the prayers of the lady and of the family. Everyone grew in faith. Jordan now had another answered prayer story to share with her class. Jordan told me later that she could not explain why, but she knew the dog was going to be all right. Perhaps the Lord put a "knowing in her knower"!

When God talks to us it is because He wants to bless us, to give us direction or to empower us. If we do not listen, He sees it as loss. He grieves. When we ignore what God is telling us, we grieve the Holy Spirit that lives inside of us. If we do not take time to listen, or if we listen but decide to be disobedient, we will eventually become numb, sometimes even justify doing the things we know "in our knower" that we are not supposed to do. We get upset with God because things did not work out the way that we wanted. All along He had been telling us that there was a better way.

Think about it this way: When God tells us through the Holy Spirit to do something, He is giving us an opportunity to make a difference in the lives of others. In order to grow in our faith, we must listen and we must be obedient.

Let me give you an example. My sister Stormy, my friend Cameron and I were eating breakfast at a restaurant one morning. We like to practice hearing from God, so we asked the Lord to tell us something about our waitress so that we might encourage her. The Lord told us that she was anxious about something that was very important to her and that she had been asking Him for money. We sensed that there was urgency about it.

When we pray in a group the Lord does not always tell each person the same thing. I find it is more like sewing a patchwork quilt together. Each person gets a piece and when each piece is in place, stitched together and completed, we can see the whole picture. We do not often see or even understand what God is doing in the beginning.

Now we could simply give the waitress a larger tip, which would have been helpful, but she would not have known the money came from God. We would have lost an opportunity to share the love of Christ with her. So we left her tip on the table. I walked to where she was in the restaurant with the other money in my hand. I touched her on the shoulder and she turned and looked me in the eyes. I said, "We were praying for you at our table this morning and the Lord told us that you needed money for something that was very important to you. We felt it was urgent that you receive this money." I put the money into her hand then continued. "The Lord loves you very much, and understands what you are going through."

With that she looked totally overwhelmed and began to cry. She said, "My daughter lives in another state and her birthday is next week. I really want to go and see her. I asked God for extra money in tips so I would have enough to get a present for her and go and see her on her birthday." She squeezed my hand and then said, "Thank you, thank you!" I took a moment to pray with her and thanked God for the blessing.

It is important that we listen to God and follow the promptings of the Holy Spirit, which works with our conscience to encourage us to do or not to do certain things. The more we have a personal relationship with God and stay connected to Him, the easier it is to hear and obey.

There are reasons why we do not hear God's voice or sometimes understand the promptings of the Holy Spirit. Sometimes we have not asked God to forgive us for the sin in our lives and sin separates us from God. Sometimes we have not dealt with generational issues. Sometimes we have hardened our hearts against Him because we are angry. Sometimes we have not spent enough time in His presence, reading His Word, being still and listening. We have become less sensitive to things in the Spirit. Or we may have been disillusioned because we were hearing and responding to the wrong voice. All of these things hinder our faith, because a walk of faith means hearing from God and responding by doing what He asks us to do.

What voice are you listening to? Let's dig a little deeper here.

Chapter Nine

FIG LEAVES, A LIAR AND THE LOUVRE

"And then she understood the devilish cunning of the enemies' plan. By mixing a little truth with it they had made their lie far stronger."

—C.S Lewis

Another voice is sometimes in our thoughts. This voice is in direct opposition to God.

When I was a young girl I loved the Lord very much and I really wanted to please Him. I was a good kid and tried to do what was expected of me. This was very difficult, however, because I lived inside my head. What I mean is, when I did anything wrong, it did not matter how big or small, I immediately went to war in my mind. I asked for forgiveness and did what I needed to do to make things right. I asked Jesus to come into my heart at least a half a dozen times when I was growing up. I wanted so much to be loved and accepted.

In my mind one sin piled on another sin and another and another until I could see myself only through the things that I had done wrong. I remember my mom telling me, "Misty, taking what didn't belong to you was wrong. It was a bad thing to do, but that doesn't mean you are a bad person. We are not what we do." I knew she was right, but I did not feel that on the inside. My mind was lost in past regrets and I had begun to let those regrets form my identity. I spent many years trying to do everything in my own strength, until one day I began to understand the truth and I began to change my mindset.

Jesus tells us that His sheep (that's us) hear His voice and will not follow anyone else (John 10:4).

> *I tell you the truth, the man who does not enter the sheep pen by the gate, but climbs in by some other way, is a thief and a robber. The one who enters by the gate is the shepherd of the sheep. The watchman opens the gate for him, and <u>the sheep listen to his voice</u>. He calls his own sheep by name and leads them out. When he has brought out all his own, he goes on ahead of them, and his sheep follow him because they know his voice. But they will never follow a <u>stranger</u>; in fact, they will run away from him because they do not recognize a stranger's voice.*
> *—John 10:1-5, NIV (emphasis mine)*

A stranger? That must mean there is someone else talking to me through my thoughts. I was learning how the Lord communicates, but at the same time it also became apparent that His voice was not the <u>only</u> one I was hearing. It was Satan, the <u>serpent</u> himself, the same one who had deceived Adam and Eve.

> *Now the <u>serpent</u> was more crafty than any of the wild animals the Lord God had made. He said to the woman, "Did God really say, 'You must not eat from any tree in the garden'?"*
> *—Genesis 3:1, NIV (emphasis mine)*

God told Adam and Eve they were free to eat from any tree in the Garden of Eden except one. The fruit of the tree of the knowledge of good and evil was off limits. If they ate the fruit from that tree they would surely <u>die</u>.

> *The Lord God took the man and put him in the Garden of Eden to work it and take care of it. And the Lord God commanded the man, "You are free to eat from any tree in the garden; but*

you must not eat from the tree of the knowledge of good and
evil, for when you eat from it you will certainly <u>die</u>."
                              —Genesis 2:15 – 16, NIV, (emphasis mine)

<u>Satan twisted what God had said</u>. He wanted Adam and Eve to question God, so he told them that they <u>would not die.</u> They would be like God, knowing good from evil. They ate the fruit and their eyes were opened. They found that what God said was true. They experienced a spiritual death. They now understood good and evil and they began to experience it. For the first time they felt shame, guilt, and condemnation. <u>They realized they were naked</u> and sewed fig leaves together to cover themselves. They tried to hide themselves in the bushes. When God spoke to them about their disobedience, they passed the buck and blamed each other.

Then the man and his wife heard the sound of the Lord God as
he was walking in the garden in the cool of the day, and they
hid from the Lord God among the trees of the garden. But the
Lord God called to the man, "Where are you?"
He answered, "I heard you in the garden, and I was afraid
because I was naked; so I hid."
And He said, "<u>Who told you that you were naked</u>? Have you
eaten from the tree that I commanded you not to eat from?"
The man said, "The woman you put here with me—she gave
me some fruit from the tree, and I ate it."
Then the Lord God said to the woman, "What is this you
have done?"
The woman said, "The serpent deceived me, and I ate."
                              —Genesis 3:8-13, NIV (emphasis mine)

"Adam was but human—this explains it all. He did
not want the apple for the apple's sake; he wanted it
only because it was forbidden. The mistake was in not

> *forbidding the serpent; then he would have eaten the serpent."*
> —Mark Twain, *Pudd'nhead Wilson*

I was struggling myself. Even if I had asked for forgiveness I was still overwhelmed with guilt, shame and condemnation. I was looking for others to blame. I wanted to share the responsibility of my sins. I did not want to face them. It is the oldest trick in the book. Satan was trying to get me to live in my past. Satan wanted me to believe that even though I had given my life to the Lord, I really was not a new person. He wanted me to believe that even though I had asked for forgiveness that I really was not forgiven. The Bible says that when we ask for forgiveness God removes the sin as <u>far as the east is from the west.</u>

> *The Lord is compassionate and gracious, slow to anger, abounding in love. He will not always accuse, nor will he harbor his anger forever; he does not treat us as our sins deserve or repay us according to our iniquities. For as high as the heavens are above the earth, so great is his love for those who fear him; <u>as far as the east is from the west</u>, so far has he removed our transgressions from us.*
> —*Psalm 103:8–12, NIV (emphasis mine)*

I love this visual picture. If I am in the east and travel toward the west going around the earth, I would never reach the west. The earth is round and we would continue endlessly around.

Satan liked to remind me of everything bad thing that I had done. I was stuck inside my head listening to the <u>liar.</u>

> *Jesus said to them, "If God were your Father, you would love me, for I came from God and now I am here. I have not come on my own; but He sent me. Why is my language not clear to you? Because you are unable to hear what I say. You belong to your father, <u>the devil</u>, and you want to carry out your father's desires. He was a murderer from the beginning, not holding to*

94

the truth, for there is no truth in him. When he lies, he speaks his native language, for <u>he is a liar and the father of lies.</u>
—John 8:42 – 44, NIV (emphasis mine)

A friend asked me to talk with a young woman whose life was paralyzed with fear (I will call her Ann). I agreed to meet Ann at a local coffee shop. She had had a difficult childhood. Her parents were alcoholics. The more they drank, the meaner and more verbally abusive they became. Ann did not feel safe at home and was fearful all of the time. She tried very hard to please them, but nothing she did was good enough. "Can't you do anything right?" they would scream.

She wanted to explain, "I did do it right!" but she could not utter the words.

They said, "You will never amount to anything! No one is ever going to love you."

She would withdraw like a turtle pulling its head into its shell. The words pierced her heart and she thought, *Is that true? Am I unlovable?* Over time these lies became her identity.

Words are powerful. Satan will take every cruel and hurtful word and make them a benchmark for our lives. A frustrated teacher says, "You are stupid! You will never get into college."

An angry sibling says, "No one likes you, you will never have a friend."

Satan wants to solidify those words inside of us like concrete. He will press lie after lie into our minds. We believe him. He is sly and says things in a way that will hurt us the most.

"They don't love me."

"I am ugly."

"I will never be the man my father wants me to be."

"No one will ever want to marry me."

"I am stupid."

"I will settle in this job because it is all I can do."

All of us have heard words like these. They are straight from the mouth of the liar! There is an adage, "Sticks and stones will break my bones but words will never harm me," (*The Christian Recorder*, March 1862, a publication of the African Methodist Episcopal Church). However, words <u>do</u> hurt! Satan knows this.

Ann had lost hope. She walled up her heart and settled into a mundane, unfulfilling job. She walked through life like a zombie. Even though she went to church, she was withdrawn and talked to no one. The Lord whispered to my friend about Ann and she went out of her way to love her. One day, Ann softened and her heart began to warm. The Holy Spirit was working from the inside.

I meet with Ann several times. I taught her about the unconditional love of Jesus and our helper called the Holy Spirit. She forgave her parents. She began replacing lie after lie with the truth. As she grew in her relationship with Christ, she began to recognize the voice of the liar. She refused to take those lies into her heart. Her life began to change. She went to college, completed her education and was hired by a good company. I heard later that she met and married a wonderful Christian man who loves her and treats her like a princess. God is so good!

Satan wants me to believe that my past is not really my past. He keeps telling me that I have no future. He tells me my circumstances are never going to change. If I think my circumstances are bad now, Satan says, just wait because they are going to get worse.

I know a man who had a perfect *Leave it to Beaver* childhood. His parents had a strong marriage and loved him unconditionally. He was an only child and got everything he ever wanted. He accomplished all of his goals, had a good paying job and a great family. This man battled within himself, however, because he felt inferior. He compared every part of his life to others. Someone always had more money than he did or a better job. He watched *Lifestyles of the Rich and Famous* and became more and more discontented. He grew disrespectful and demanding at work. He got angry and saw himself as inferior to those around him. Pretty soon the wonderful life he had was not good enough. Instead of taking his wishes and dreams to God, he became bitter and poisoned everything around him. He eventually lost his job and his family. He had fallen into Satan's trap.

Satan lies about what other people say and think and feel about us. Satan wants us to keep our eyes on what we do not have, instead of on what we have. Liar, liar, pants on fire! When we believe a lie, we empower the liar. I was actually giving Satan power over my life. I knew the truth of the Bible, but I was not living it. It was not a heart experience; it was all in my head. The only way to counteract a lie is by understanding the truth and walking it out.

"How you respond to the enemy of your soul determines whether his plan for your life or God's plan for your life is realized."

—Stormie Omartian, *Prayer Warrior*

The scripture says that if any man is in Christ then he is a <u>new creation</u>. Old things have passed away and all things have become new.

Therefore, if anyone is in Christ, he is a <u>new creation</u>; the old has gone, the new has come!
—2 Corinthians 5:17, NIV (emphasis mine)

From the moment we accept Jesus as our Savior, we are no longer the same people on the inside. We are the way Adam and Eve were before they ate the apple and our nature was corrupted. Before there was guilt, shame, condemnation, religion, or a works mentality. We must see ourselves separated from our sin. We are totally different. We are new creatures who have been <u>crucified with Christ</u>.

I have been <u>crucified with Christ</u> and I no longer live, but Christ lives in me. The life I live in the body, I live by faith in the Son of God, who loved me and gave himself for me.
—Galatians 2:20, NIV (emphasis mine)

Oh, we still know all about our sinful nature and struggle with it. <u>Satan will not let us forget.</u> He does not want us to believe that we are different than we were before we were saved. He tricks us and tells us lies and tempts us with things that lead us right into sin—just like a donkey following a carrot.

Simon, Simon, Satan has asked to <u>sift you as wheat</u>. But I have prayed for you, Simon, that your faith may not fail. And when you have turned back, strengthen your brothers.
—Luke 22:31, NIV (emphasis mine)

We get the filth of the world on us and it feels as though it has become a part of us. We feel we are not new. Satan deceives us and fills our minds with criticism, condemnation and lies to us about how we are failures. He tries to steal our identity. If we forget who we are in Christ, we walk into the prison that Satan has waiting for us.

Our past is literally our past. It means that we are no longer who we used to be. We are not our old nature or those things that we did. Jesus is not into time-shares. The Holy Spirit does not want to live in the condo with our old nature. He has already purchased the entire building. We are not simply reformed, re-educated or rehabilitated. We are re-created! When we trust Christ, we exchange our sin for His righteousness. What an amazing gift!

We must completely change the way we look at ourselves. The way we see ourselves should be an accurate picture of what Christ has done for us. If we do not see ourselves in the way we should and if we do not forgive ourselves, we are basically denying the work that Jesus accomplished for us on the cross. Jesus does not want us to walk around beating ourselves up for things that He took care of with His shed blood. If we do not see ourselves as new creatures then we hold ourselves back from confidently living out who we really are in Christ. We will be hesitant to approach the Father because we will feel unworthy.

"We may not pay Satan reverence, for that would be indiscreet, but we can at least respect his talents."
—Mark Twain

Think about it this way. Let's say that you have always wanted to go to Paris, France. Then someone who loves you decides to bless you by giving you the trip. So he gets airline tickets, makes hotel reservations, arranges for car rental, makes reservations in the nicest restaurants. He even gets tickets to the Louvre for you. Everything is taken care of and paid for in advance. A new wardrobe has been purchased for you and packed for the trip. He even squared it with your boss so you can go. A limo pulls up to your front door to take you to the airport. You refuse to get into the car because you do not believe that what has been given to you is real. That does not make much sense, does it?

When we receive a gift the giver is glad, filled with joy and is glorified. If not, then we mock the giver and make him feel unappreciated. That is what we do to God when we do not receive His gift!

We are not our feelings. Feelings come from our soul and can be corrupted. Experiencing an emotion is not a sin. The emotion is not wrong. We should always let our emotions direct us toward something good, toward the truth.

We cannot fight this by sheer will and determination. Satan is a master in this game. We fight by getting in the Word and learning the truth. We <u>cast down every imagination</u> that does not line up with the word of God. We fight it by speaking the truth out of our mouths and coming into agreement with it. We fight it by <u>rebuking Satan</u> and coming against every evil thing that sets itself against the Word of God.

> *The Lord said to Satan, "The Lord <u>rebuke you</u>, Satan! The Lord, who has chosen Jerusalem, rebuke you! Is not this man a burning stick snatched from the fire?"*
> *—Zechariah 3:2, NIV (emphasis mine)*

We <u>cast down any imagination</u> that does not line up with the Word of God.

> *I beg you that when I come I may not have to be as bold as I expect to be toward some people who think that we live by the standards of this world. For though we live in the world, we do not wage war as the world does. The weapons we fight with are not the weapons of the world. On the contrary, they have divine power to demolish strongholds. We demolish arguments and every pretension that sets itself up against the knowledge of God, and <u>we take captive every thought</u> to make it obedient to*

Christ. And we will be ready to punish every act of disobedience,
once your obedience is complete.
　　　　　　　　　　—2 Corinthians 10:2-6, NIV (emphasis mine)

My sister Stormy is strong, courageous and bold. She is smart, educated, and very talented. She knows her way around a computer. She remodels houses and is a gifted artist. She has an unwavering faith in God and has accomplished every goal she has set for herself. She amazes me.

Stormy was talking with the Lord one day and said, "Lord, thank you that I do not live my life in fear."

He said, "If that is true then why are you worried about your future?"

Ouch! God knew her heart. Her mind was always filled with questions.

"Am I going to have enough money when I get old?"

"Where is the money going to come from?"

"Where am I going to live?"

"Who is going to take care of me?"

Her sleep was fitful as she dwelled on these things. Satan had her bound. Instead of trusting God, she had picked up the burden of her future provisions and carried it like a millstone around her neck. This worry left her feeling fearful and helpless.

Stormy repented. She turned to God for help. She asked the Lord to give her strategies and ideas to help her make money. God presented her with opportunities to buy houses at rock bottom prices. She used her remodeling and decorating talents and began flipping houses. She loves to see them transformed into beautiful homes. She now owns several rental properties and has a sense of peace. God is faithful!

The Lord has great things in mind for us. We should look at things from the His perspective, and not from our own or the world's perspective. How we see ourselves and knowing who we are in Christ is fundamental if we are going to become all He created us to be.

Although we recognize these things with our minds, it is more of a heart issue, not a head issue. When we have the thought that we are worthless, we must do more than go into self-promotion or work to make ourselves acceptable. We must recognize that it is the stranger's voice and we are not to follow. It is a command. We must replace the lie with the truth! "Lord, I thank you that I am yours and you are mine. I am worth so much to you that you gave your life for me and I am precious in your sight. I am humbled by how you love me unconditionally. Satan has no authority and I refuse to give him any place in my life. My life is a celebration! In Jesus' Name, amen." The truth needs to settle deep inside us.

"Satan is so much more in earnest than we are—he buys up the opportunity while we are wondering how much it will cost."

—Amy Carmichael

We make the decision to cast down everything that exalts itself against the knowledge of God. We bring every evil, ungodly thought into captivity. Satan wants us to believe the thought that we had about being worthless is true. He wants us to believe that we are still who we used to be. He will tell us who we are not. If we believe it, then we give Satan a foothold into our lives. The more we feel badly about the past, the more we do not want to receive the Father's love. We should be able to look in a mirror at ourselves and honestly but humbly say, "I love you!" and mean it. Our hearts and minds should be so focused on Jesus Christ and on who we are in Him that everything else loses its voice. We must act on the Word in order to experience it. If we want to know how we are doing in this area, we must look at how we are responding.

Satan does not want us to walk in faith and have a victorious life. His mission is to steal, kill, and destroy (John 10:10) and he will use any trickery or means to do it.

"It was a costly triumph. But God's values are not so easily reckoned. If God had simply terminated Satan, then it would not have been so clear that God is both stronger and infinitely more to be desired than Satan. God wills for his glory to shine forth not only through

acts of physical power, but also through acts of moral and spiritual power that display the beauty of his grace with lavish colors. To take sinners out of Satan's hands by virtue of Christ's sin-bearing sacrifice and his law-fulfilling obedience to the Father was a more glorious victory than mere annihilation of the enemy."
        —John Piper, *Seeing and Savoring Jesus Christ*

Chapter Ten

A Tomato, Journals, and a Closed Door

"Within the covers of the Bible are the answers for all the problems men face."

—Ronald Reagan

God wants to give us the desires of our hearts. He reminded me of this on a hot Saturday afternoon when I was in Africa. I was craving a tomato. Fruits and vegetables were very scarce in the area where I lived so I did not eat them very often. My mouth watered just thinking about eating a big, red, juicy tomato. As I prepared to go and visit a village that morning I prayed, "Lord I would like a big, ripe tomato. Thanks for sending one to me." I had no idea how He would answer that prayer since I had not seen a tomato since I had been there, but I knew He would.

The pastors and I arrived at the village and walked down a well-worn path toward a tree where we were going to meet the people from the village. About that time, a woman walked out of the bush carrying a bowl of the prettiest tomatoes on top of her head. I could hardly believe what I was seeing. The lady was happy to sell them. I thanked God and then ate a tomato whole, like an apple. It was delicious!

God wants us to know Him. To <u>know</u> means to understand through experience. We have the mind of Christ (1 Corinthians 3:16). When Adam and Eve disobeyed God, they walked away from God's <u>way</u> of doing things. They sabotaged their destiny, forfeited His provision and stepped out of His protection.

> *Praise the Lord, O my soul; all my inmost being, praise His Holy Name. Praise the Lord, O my soul, and forget not all His benefits—who forgives all your sins and heals all your diseases, who redeems your life from the pit and crowns you with love and compassion, who satisfies your desires with good thing so that your youth is renewed like the eagle's. The Lord works righteousness and justice for all oppressed. He <u>made known</u> His <u>ways</u> to Moses, His <u>deeds</u> to the people of Israel: The Lord is compassionate and gracious, slow to anger, abounding in love.*
> *—Psalm 103:1-8 (emphasis mine)*

It is interesting that God made His <u>ways</u> known to Moses but only his <u>deeds</u> to the people of Israel. To know God means knowing His ways or the <u>way He does things</u> (Deuteronomy 10:12-13). God wants us to honor His commandments and to be obedient. His commandments are meant to bless us and should not be a burden (Joshua 22:5).

> *To know God means knowing His thoughts or what He thinks*
> *—(1 Corinthians 2:16)*

The more we know how He thinks, the more we will trust Him. This empowers our faith. He will guide us into truth so we will not be deceived.

To know God means knowing His <u>desires</u> or what He feels (Psalm 103:15-18). When God thinks of us, He has great things in mind. If we know how much He loves us and if we believe we can trust Him, this will keep us holy and away from corruption.

To know God means knowing <u>what we can expect </u>from Him. We can even expect little things like receiving a tomato or vegetable soup. How do we get to know Him? By communicating with Him. The Lord speaks to us directly through the Holy Spirit, as I mentioned earlier, but He will also speak to us through the Word of God, the Bible. One time I was faced with making a decision about moving to another area. It would literally change my whole world. The Lord directed me to scripture, which reassured me that He would give me wisdom and I would know what to do. We must believe and not doubt.

> *If any of you lacks wisdom, he should ask God, who gives generously to all without finding fault, and it will be given to you. But when he asks he must believe and not doubt, because he who doubts is like a wave of the sea, blown and tossed by the wind. That man should not think he will receive anything from the Lord; he is double-minded and unstable in all he does.*
> *—James 1:5-8, NIV (emphasis mine)*

He also reminded me that He was able to do more than I could ask or imagine. I have been given the power to do what I need to do.

> *Now to him who is able to do immeasurably more than all we ask or imagine, according to his power that is at work within us...*
> *—Ephesians 3:20, NIV (emphasis mine)*

He encouraged me that He would meet every need I had.

> *And my God will meet all your needs according to His Glorious riches in Christ Jesus.*
> *—Philippians 4:10, NIV (emphasis mine)*

God says He will watch over His Word to perform it. God will not budge when it comes to His Word. I decided to take Him at His Word and I am so glad that I did! Moving was the right thing to do. I find the best way to receive encouragement from the Lord is by spending time regularly with Him studying the Bible. I like the way Helen spent time with the Lord. She taught me how to have a quiet time.

*Go now, <u>write it</u> on a tablet for them, inscribe it on a scroll, that
for the days to come it may be an everlasting witness.*
$\qquad$ —*Isaiah 30:8, NIV (emphasis mine)*

She had me write instructions and the scripture from Isaiah in the
front of my first <u>journal.</u> When she taught me how to have a quiet time
she said, "If you ever quit journaling, the instructions will always be
there for you to go back to." Helen gave journals and devotion books to
me. She was living by faith, yet she provided them for years. I have an
old devotion book that she used so often that it is falling apart. It is full
of her personal notes and markings in different colored pens. I cherish
it! We started by using a devotion book. Helen loved *Streams in the
Desert: Volume One* or *My Utmost for His Highest* or *Daily Light From
the Bible*, to name a few. Each devotion book had a primary verse. We
would never read the devotion first. That should never be the focus. We
would go straight to the Bible and read the whole chapter of the verse
that was in the devotion book. We would pray over the scripture and
ask the Lord to teach us through it. How did it apply to our lives now?
What are we to do with the information? We wrote everything down
in our journals. Only then would we read from the devotion book. We
followed suit and wrote how that applied to us as well.

Reading through the Bible is important, also. So we would go back
to the last place that we were reading in our Bible and read a chapter
or two, depending upon how much time we had. I call this digging in
the Word because it is similar to treasure hunting. With a good study
Bible it is like following clues. Something that I read sparks a question
and then I follow the references and footnotes and pretty soon I am
lost in this world of divine revelation. The discovery never ends. It fits
my personality. I love figuring things out and discovering truth. The
Word is filled with truth!

The Lord also speaks through other people. As a matter of fact, we
are to seek out <u>Godly counsel</u>.

*The way of fools seems right to them, but the wise <u>listen
to advice</u>.*
$\qquad$ —*Proverbs 12:15, NIV (emphasis mine)*

It is not always easy to find Godly counsel, is it? We should choose someone who is a person of wisdom and integrity and who hears from the Lord.

One time a lady came to me and asked for prayer. She was in the middle of a conflict and did not know how to solve it without hurting someone's feelings. She had talked with three people. Each person had given her a different solution. If she had listened to her friends, she would have lied, betrayed a confidence or turned her back on people she loved. None of those solutions seemed right to her. She hated confrontation, but eventually faced her fears and arranged to meet with those in the middle of the conflict. She spoke the truth in love and the whole misunderstanding was resolved in no time. Any time we make a decision that goes against the principles in the Word of God, we are making a bad decision.

"Sometimes the Bible in the hand of one man is worse than a whisky bottle in the hand of (another)... There are just some kind of men who're so busy worrying about the next world they've never learned to live in this one, and you can look down the street and see the results."

—Harper Lee, *To Kill a Mockingbird*

Sometimes the simplest things the Lord does through people are the most helpful. Once I was feeling overwhelmed with the responsibilities that I was facing and someone I did not know gave me a Bible verse.

She said, "I know you don't know me, but in my quiet time this morning the Lord gave me this scripture to encourage you." She had no idea how much I needed that confirmation at that very moment.

The Lord also speaks through situations and circumstances. A friend came into my office one day very upset. She had been praying for a while about getting a certain job she really wanted. It seemed to be an upwardly mobile business and she thought she would do well in that job. She interviewed, but they had decided to give it to someone else. She was disappointed and questioned the Lord about it. I told her there had to be a reason for it and she should not be discouraged. I believed it meant that the Lord had something even better for her.

It is tough when we pray and the answer is no and we do not know why. We may never know about some things.

A short time later she was hired to work for a company and she loved it! She fit well with them and really felt as though she was making a difference there. A few months after that we read in the paper that the business she had wanted to work for originally had come under investigation for allegations of fraud. If that company had employed her, she would have been embroiled in a mess. The Lord had interrupted her plans. Sometimes a "no" answer from the Lord and a closed door will turn out to be the best thing for us.

"We were given the Scriptures to humble us into realizing that God is right, and the rest of us are just guessing."
—Rich Mullins

We become disillusioned when we look around and see that God has answered the prayers of other people, when He has not answered our prayers. It can be downright discouraging. Answered prayer is rarely as simple as it seems. There is usually a story there about how long a person had to wait or about closed door after closed door before the right door was opened. God can be frustratingly slow. Sometimes God will not change our circumstances right away, but will give us what we need to carry on. Or, like my friend in the story, sometimes we will even lose something we thought was good before God provides something excellent.

If God does not answer our prayer, it does not mean we have failed or done something wrong. We only fail if we stop praying. Lazarus died and Martha held on to her faith. "Lord," Martha said to Jesus, "if you had been here, my brother would not have died. But I know that even now God will give you whatever you ask," (John 11:21-22, NIV emphasis mine). Martha knew that the Lord could answer the prayer for her brother, "even now." Lazarus was resurrected. We should have "even now" faith. Elijah prayed for rain and sent a servant seven times to see if the rains were coming (1 Kings 18). Elijah did not give up. The rain came in a flood! God sees the whole picture and knows what is best for us. We must be encouraged and pray hard. We should not stop praying, ever!

We usually stop praying when we run out of things to say. We feel as though our prayers are hitting a brass ceiling and getting nowhere. When this happens we should pray the scripture. When we pray the Word of God, the Word will become a part of us. When we are praying the scripture aloud, we read a verse; it resonates in our spirits and encourages us. It will bolster our faith. We can also use the Word and remind God of what He has done in the past.

Once when I lived in Africa, we experienced a drought in a certain region. The pastors came and asked me to pray for rain. We prayed together, "Lord if you brought the rain for Elijah, you will bring the rain for us!" The rains came, but something even more amazing happened. It only rained on the fields planted by members of their churches. Our prayers were not that specific, but God knew what He was doing.

People noticed and asked, "Why is it raining on your field and not mine when my field is right next to yours?"

The farmers replied, "We asked Jesus to make it rain and He did."

Astonished, they responded, "Who is this Jesus? Who is this man who brings the rain? We want to know this Jesus!" Countless people became followers of Jesus that day and the rain came for them, too. There was an abundant harvest. The churches were full the following Sunday!

Peace comes when we turn everything over to the Lord and keep praying. When we feel anxious it is difficult to discern His still small voice. Anxiety leads to insecurity. The Lord died on the cross so we could have peace and security. Once we understand what He did for us, we gain confidence and became audacious in our actions! Faith and audacity go hand in hand.

"Out of 100 men, one will read the Bible, the other 99 will read the Christian."

—D.L. Moody

Chapter Eleven

CHOCOLATE, A MAILBOX AND A PEARL RING

"She can take the most complicated things in life and wrap them up so small and simple, they'll fit right in your pocket."

—Kathryn Stockett, *The Help*

To walk in faith, one must maintain a place of rest on the inside. It is easier said then done. In order to live in peace, we must first approach God with a repentant heart and be committed to Him and to His will. We must be settled in the fact that we have been redeemed and are now His children. These things will lead to a "<u>peace, which transcends understanding</u>."

> *Do not be anxious about anything, but in everything, by prayer and petition, with thanksgiving, present your requests to God. And the <u>peace of God, which transcends all understanding</u>, will guard your hearts and your minds in Christ Jesus.*
> *—Philippians 4:6-7, NIV (emphasis mine)*

What is peace? Stripping it down to the bare bones, peace is about having our questions answered. Our thoughts become overrun with questions we wish the Lord would settle for us.

> I am sick. Are You going to heal me?
> How are You going to heal me?
> When are You going to heal me?
> Where will I get the money I need?
> I have been falsely accused. What am I going to do about it?
> Will my children be safe?
> What is going to happen in my future?
> Am I going to be secure in my old age?
> Millions of things we face every day may push us into anxiety.

The world might define peace as lack of conflict, war, noise or turmoil. While I am sure that is true, I believe peace or rest is different for Christians. It is not about the lack of something; it is about the presence of something. It is about experiencing daily the presence of the Holy Spirit as He involves Himself in every situation in our lives. Storms and conflicts do happen; we live in a broken world filled with broken people. Being aware of the presence of the Holy Spirit brings us peace on the inside, and helps us weather the storms that are happening on the outside.

This scripture says we should worry about nothing. If we seek God first, He will take care of everything for us. There will be no need to worry because we can trust Him.

> *Therefore I tell you, do not worry about your life, what you will eat or drink; or about your body, what you will wear. Is not life more than food, and the body more than clothes? Look at the birds of the air; they do not sow or reap or store away in barns, and yet your heavenly Father feeds them. Are you not much more valuable than they? Can any one of you by worrying add a single hour to your life? And why do you worry about clothes? See how the flowers of the field grow. They do not labor or spin. Yet I tell you that not even Solomon in all his splendor was dressed like one of these. If that is how God clothes the grass*

of the field, which is here today and tomorrow is thrown into the fire, will he not much more clothe you—you of little faith? So do not worry, saying, 'What shall we eat?' or 'What shall we drink?' or 'What shall we wear?' For the pagans run after all these things, and your heavenly Father knows that you need them. <u>But seek first his kingdom</u> and his righteousness, and all these things will be given to you as well. Therefore do not worry about tomorrow, for tomorrow will worry about itself. Each day has enough trouble of its own.

—Matthew 6:25-34, NIV (emphasis mine)

The word "nothing" in Webster's dictionary means, "Not anything or no thing." That eliminates everything. We are to pray about everything. We should tell God literally everything that is on our hearts and minds.

> If we talk to Him about our fears,
>> He will help us deal with them.
>
> If we give Him our troubles,
>> He will help and comfort us.
>
> If we celebrate our pleasures in life,
>> He will rejoice with us.
>
> If we share our desires with Him,
>> He will refine them and empower us.
>
> If we surrender our difficulties,
>> He will help us conquer them.
>
> If we reveal our temptations,
>> He will shield us and teach us to overpower them.
>
> If we show Him our wounds,
>> He will heal them.
>
> If we admit our indifference,
>> He will prick our hearts.
>
> If we recognize that our selfishness has made us unjust,
>> He will redirect our focus.
>
> If we realize that our vanity leads to insecurity,
>> He will keep us from hiding behind it.

The key is to hold nothing back. If we pause to weigh or reconsider our words, for any reason, before we say them then we are not being real with God. We talk with our best friend about everything because we do not keep any secrets from him. We are not afraid that we will be judged, so we are totally honest and transparent. My friend Helen lived a life of divine encounter because she had daily, unreserved, divine conversations with God!

A pastor I met shared this story with me. Several years ago, he was in a plane flying from the United Kingdom to Ghana. There were three seats together on the plane. The woman who was sitting by the window was visibly shaken. She was dressed as if she had not taken the time to think about her attire. Tears ran down her face for the longest time as she prayed. The pastor was sitting on the aisle seat but gained courage to talk to the woman, even though he was talking over the man sitting in the middle.

The young woman had been living in the United Kingdom for ten years and had a nice place to live. She was very successful, but was now being deported. The paperwork for her visa renewal was so tied up in red tape that it expired without her knowing. Government officials picked her up without notice, took her to the airport and put her on a plane back to her own country. She wept while telling him that she was going home with nothing. She did not have a pound sterling to her name. She did not even have clothes. She was distraught, crying out to God. She did not know what she was going to do. She was embarrassed about going back to her family under these conditions. The pastor did not know what to say, but encouraged her. He prayed with her.

The man sitting between them listened quietly. As the plane was landing the man said, "The same thing happened to me one time. I know what you are going through." He opened his wallet and gave the women a large amount of money. He said, "You go home and do not tell anyone what has happened to you. First, you go and buy some good clothes. Clean yourself and dress. Then go and get the nicest place to live that you can find. Here is my contact information. If you need anything else, get in touch with me."

The pastor checked on her from time to time. The women had gotten in touch with the man who had showered her with generosity. They eventually fell in love and got married. She is now the CEO of one of his companies in the United Kingdom. It turns out that he is a multi-millionaire, owning several companies in the UK and other countries. She bared her soul to the Lord and held nothing back. God honored her. She left with nothing and returned as a queen. Isn't that just like God?

We must approach God with <u>repentant hearts</u>. A troubled young couple talked with me about their twelve year old daughter (I will call her Beth). They were at their wits end! Beth was constantly in trouble. She had misbehaved so badly at school that the administration threatened to permanently expel her. She was disrespectful. She dressed provocatively and chased after older boys. Her parents were frightened for her and for her future. They had tried counseling and punishment. Nothing worked. They had loved and encouraged her. They knew she had deep emotional issues, but simply did not know what to do. After I talked with Beth, one of the things she told me explained so much.

Beth flippantly said, "I know what I am doing is wrong, but I don't care. It is fun and I am going to keep doing what I want to do! Besides, all I have to do is ask Jesus to forgive me and He has to forgive me."

Whoa! That is like saying, "I'm going to say the sinners' prayer and pretend to commit my life to Christ because I need a little fire insurance. I'll do it so it will keep me from the fires of hell." Prayer does not work that way. We must have repentant hearts. The Lord knows if we are being sincere!

Beth had been in church long enough to learn that God forgives. She was using God's gift of forgiveness to justify her behavior. After spending many hours with her, she learned to approach God and her parents with humility. With her now repentant heart her prayers were sincere. Her behavior changed and she became someone her parents could be proud of. It is comforting to know that if we sin, we do not have to live with the heavy weight of it. Jesus made a way out for us if we sincerely repent and ask for forgiveness. We can live at peace.

Then there is the <u>rest that redemption brings</u>.

In him we have <u>redemption</u> through his blood, the forgiveness of sins, in accordance with the riches of God's grace that he lavished on us with all wisdom and understanding. And He

made known to us the mystery of his will according to his good pleasure, which he purposed in Christ...
—Ephesians 1:7-9, NIV (emphasis mine)

Redemption is a gift that Christ gave to us. We have been redeemed and now can be at peace because we are His children. Here is a simple way to explain redemption. Let's say that you have a big craving for chocolate. So you go to the store, pick up a candy bar, pay for it and take it with you. You have redeemed the candy bar. You exchanged money for the chocolate.

We are like that candy bar; we have been redeemed. The Lord pointed at us and told God, "This is My child and I love her! I am going to trade My life for My child." And He did and so we are His. We did not have a say in it. He freely gave His life for us. If we choose to let Jesus be the center of our lives, then we can <u>rest</u> in the fact that He loves us unconditionally and He will always be there to sustain us.

Helen, my mentor and friend, told me a wonderful story about redemption.

She began:

I got a phone call one day from the person who was in charge of the students at Chalkville. He asked me if I would come to the school because they needed me. When I arrived I learned that a fifteen-year-old boy had beaten a matron so severely in a fit of rage that she was in the hospital. He had been locked up. I thought, *Lord, what am I supposed to do? I can tell that everyone here is afraid of him.*

Then they asked me if I would go in and talk to him. They had to unlock and then lock three doors before I would be in his cell. I knew that if he lost his temper or went into a rage while I was there I would be in trouble. I prayed and the Lord told me to go in and that He would tell me what to do. They unlocked all of the doors and I went in. The boy jumped up from the bed and stood against the wall defensively with clinched fists. I sat on the edge of the bed and said, 'I have two things to tell you. The first is that Jesus loves you very much. The second is that I love you very much.' The boy sat down on the bed and began to cry. He said, 'You are the first person who has ever told me they love me.' I talked with him for a while and then led him to the Lord right there.

For the first time in his life, this young boy began to understand the meaning of unconditional love. He went from feeling alone to knowing His heavenly Father was always with Him. Instead of struggling alone, he understood the Lord was there to help him. He went from hopeless to hopeful. The experience changed his life.

Think of it this way: God chose us and we chose Him. We are now yoked together. Jesus wants to carry all of our <u>burdens</u>. He is gentle and will help us find <u>rest</u> for our souls. Look at what Jesus said.

> *Come to me, all you who are weary and <u>burdened</u>, and I will give you <u>rest</u>. Take my <u>yoke</u> upon you and learn from me, for I am gentle and humble in heart, and you will find rest for your souls. For my yoke is easy and my burden is light.*
> *—Matthew 11:29-30, NIV (emphasis mine)*

He will help us with our every day needs, which can be a burden to us, but there is more to it than that. Jesus also took the burden of our sin upon Himself. Sin is too heavy for us to carry. We can choose to be yoked with him.

Years ago, in order to plow a field a farmer harnessed two oxen together using a yoke before attaching a plow. If the oxen were equally yoked they walked side by side and plowed a straight row. If they were unequally yoked, the oxen pulled against one another. To be yoked with Christ means we are moving in the same direction and not fighting against Him. There is a <u>rest</u> that comes when we are <u>committed to Christ</u> and <u>obedient to His will</u>.

> *Jesus replied, "Anyone who loves me, will <u>obey</u> my teaching. My Father will love him, and we will come to him and make our home with him. He who does not love me will not obey my teaching. These words you hear are not my own; they belong to the Father who sent me.*
> *"All this I have spoken while still with you. But the <u>Counselor, the Holy Spirit</u>, whom the Father will send in my name, will teach you all things and will remind you of everything I have said to you. Peace I leave with you; my peace I give you. I do*

not give to you as the world gives. <u>Do not let your hearts be troubled and do not be afraid</u>."

—John 14:23-27, NIV (emphasis mine)

The peace Jesus mentions is tranquility. It is the peace we feel when we see a beautiful sunset. We feel tranquil when we have talked with our family members and they are well. There is a peace we have when we come away from a time of prayer. We have a calm assurance that everything is fine. He has given us the Holy Spirit, our helper and, if we receive it, everything else we need.

"God wants to lead you to places you cannot get to without Him, and He does that by the power of His Spirit. He can bring you into the realm of the miraculous— not as a show, but as a demonstration of His love and compassion for the lost, hurting, or needy. Who among us doesn't want or need that?"

—Stormie Omartian

A sad, young wife visited me one day and asked me to pray with her. She had lost her peace and was filled with regret. Her husband was unfaithful and walked away from the marriage. She was devastated, as you might imagine. She had always been faithful and thought they had a good marriage. The rejection was more than she could take. She began to feel insecure and needy. She craved love and acceptance. It was not long before she found herself in the arms of someone she did not love or even care about. She gave herself completely to him. Knowing this was not the Christian thing to do, she was overwhelmed with guilt and too ashamed to turn to the Lord.

"A man should never be ashamed to own that he has been in the wrong, which is but saying... that he is wiser today than yesterday."

—Jonathan Swift

When we disappoint someone we have a tendency to avoid that person altogether. We judge ourselves, so we feel they will judge us as well. If we are honest and give people a chance, they usually will not respond in the way we expect. We treat God the same way. We avoid Him when He is the very one who can help us the most. We have been redeemed, accepted, justified, and forgiven. We should then turn boldly to God without shame or fear. Shame, fear, guilt and condemnation are tools of Satan.

When we are at peace, we will be able to handle life's challenges. When the Lord communicates, we will have clarity and a better discernment of Spirit. Faith is easy when peace is there.

"Some people think they have discernment when actually they are just suspicious. Suspicion comes out of the unrenewed mind; discernment comes out of the renewed spirit."

—Joyce Meyer,
Battlefield of the Mind:
Winning the Battle in Your Mind

I mentioned earlier that my sister Stormy lived across the hall on the second floor of the same apartment building as my friend Helen. One day, Stormy watched as Helen went downstairs and toward her mailbox. She stopped halfway, however, threw her head back and laughed, before turning around and going back upstairs. When Helen reached the top of the stairwell, Stormy asked her why she was laughing.

Helen said, "He said it wasn't in there!"

Stormy asked, "What's not in where?"

Helen said, "My social security check. The Lord said it wasn't in the mailbox."

Helen went back to her apartment and she told me later about the conversation she had with the Lord. She said:

I prayed, "Now Lord, my rent is due right now and I am counting on getting that social security check so I can pay my rent." He asked, "Helen, who is your provider?" She said, "You are, Lord." He said,

"That's right and that check will not be in that mailbox until I want it to be in that mailbox."

Helen's only income was a very small social security check. She lived by faith. Her life verse was *Isaiah 54:5 (NIV): "For your Maker is your husband, The Lord Almighty is His name; the Holy One of Israel is your redeemer, He is called the God of all the earth."*

Helen said, "Christ is my husband. Do you know what a husband's responsibility is?"

I said, "A husband should provide for and protect the family. Love them unconditionally. Discipline the children and encourage them to do things well. Lead the family in the ways of God. Participate in things that are going on in their lives. Patiently listen and give wise council. Take responsibility at home; perhaps repair things that are broken. Is that right?"

"Yes," she said. "That is what I can expect from Jesus!" She smiled so big it pulled her glasses closer up on her nose.

When Helen began to get worried or fretful, she would remind herself that it was the Lord's job to take care of her. She even wore a pearl ring on her left ring finger as a reminder. Helen knew "her Maker was her husband."

Her social security check was not delivered for another two weeks, yet her rent and every bill she had was paid! She prayed without ceasing and was completely at peace the entire time. Money was slipped under her door, handed to her or it came in the mail. She never asked anyone for money. Every need was met and she was not anxious. She knew the Lord would provide as He promised. Helen lived in that wonderful place of total trust and peace. She was so at peace that if someone needed her last fifty dollars, she would give it to him knowing God would provide for her.

We should be determined to pray until we see the thing that we are praying for. This prayer leads to self-sacrifice. It means being consistent and not taking no for an answer. This kind of prayer is more than repetitive words. This prayer is intense, moves us deeply and takes us right to the heart of God.

"God is God. Because he is God, He is worthy of my trust and obedience. I will find rest nowhere but in His holy will that is unspeakably beyond my largest notions of what he is up to."

—Elisabeth Elliot

Chapter Twelve

TOOTHPASTE, RED LOBSTER AND A THUMPER MARBLE

"Does it make sense to pray for guidance about the future if we are not obeying in the thing that lies before us today? How many momentous events in Scripture depended on one person's seemingly small act of obedience! Rest assured: Do what God tells you to do now, and, depend upon it, you will be shown what to do next."

—Elisabeth Elliot,
Quest for Love: True Stories of Passion and Purity

We can have a great relationship with Jesus, spend time studying His Word, and even walk in peace. We will be paralyzed, however, if we are disobedient.

Everyone who knows her will tell you that my mother, Eva Carter Hicks, is an amazing person. She has tremendous strength. People buttonhole her everywhere she goes because she is a great listener and teacher. She is incredibly wise. Mom taught me the importance of obedience. She also taught my siblings and me the value of hard work. When we were children and began to grumble about our chores, she would say, "Just work five minutes more." As we worked, five minutes turned into ten minutes. Ten minutes turned into twenty minutes. Before we knew it, an hour had passed and the project was completed. We felt good about the work we had done.

She had a saying, "If a task is once begun, never leave it till it's done. Be thy labor great or small, do it well or not at all!" She meant it, too. We would do our chores well and in a timely fashion or we would do them over again. Delayed obedience is disobedience. She rewarded us when we did well, but also let us know what we could expect if we did not do as we were told. Mom was fair, set great boundaries and always followed through. We knew that she loved us, and we could trust her, so we felt very safe. She instilled in us a great work ethic. I am very thankful for that. It has helped me in life, but also in my relationship with the Lord. What does that have to do with faith or spirituality? Everything!

Christians are disciples of Jesus. To be a disciple means giving up our right to ourselves. As Christians we probably said something like, "Lord, my life is yours. Tell me what to do and I will do it." If we are sincere about that, then we must be obedient and freely participate in what God is doing. God, in His great wisdom, presents opportunities to us that move us forward in life and in our relationship with Him.

Obedience always starts with little things. One of the elementary children at church asked, "Can I play with the toys in one of the Sunday school rooms while you meet with my mom?" His mom was a volunteer leader in our children's ministry.

I said, "Sure you can, but please put all of the toys away no later than 4:00 when our meeting will be finished." I pointed to the clock on the wall. He agreed.

We concluded the meeting and went across the hall. We found him flipping through the pages of a children's Bible. The room was a mess!

I said, "The room is a mess. You promised you would have everything put away by four o'clock. What happened?"

He said, "I am reading the Bible instead."

Our leaders always emphasize the importance of reading the Bible each time the children gather in church. He was hoping to use it as an excuse for not doing what he was supposed to do.

I said, "I am happy that you are reading the Bible, but that is not what your mom and I asked you to do, is it?"

He said, "No, ma'am." He begrudgingly got up and put the toys away. It was a good teaching moment.

"Israel's first king, Saul, looked like he was born for the role. He was tall, handsome, intelligent, and sensitive to God's leading. But he eventually lost most of his attractive qualities, the most important being obedience."

—Charles R. Swindoll

Character is shaped by obedience. Character is very important to God. Godly righteousness and character are built in us when we stop striving and give ourselves completely to His will. The things the Lord asks us to do are precious to him. He needs us to be faithful and true. Do we have a Godly character? Can He trust us?

The Bible says obedience is better than sacrifice (1 Samuel 15:22). Sometimes we sacrifice what is excellent for something that is only good. We fill our lives with things that are good instead of doing as God instructs. We miss something greater. We miss the opportunity to have much richer life experiences. God created us and then gave us the ability to disobey. Extraordinary! To truly make a difference, a demand must be placed upon us before others will see what the Lord will do for us or through us. The quiet response that we make toward what is required of us always reveals our character and commitment.

When the Lord talks to us there is a reason for it. He does not simply talk about nonsense all day to fill the time. He has bigger things in mind. There is a reason behind everything that He does. What He has in mind is always <u>what is best for us,</u> no matter what that may look like.

For the Lord God is a sun and shield; The Lord bestows favor and honor, <u>No good thing does He withhold</u> from those whose walk is blameless.

—Psalm 84:11, NIV (emphasis mine)

I watched my friend Helen closely for weeks, then months, then years. She chose to be obedient, and did everything the Lord asked her to do. The freedom to choose is a wonderful gift from God. The Lord is a gentleman and never forces us to do what we do not want to do. We are not all robots, mindlessly doing God's bidding. There is no love in that. We would not love someone who treated us like slaves. Think of it this way. God is taking us on a wonderful, incredible journey, one that will fulfill and satisfy. It is important to trust the one who is making the journey with us, even if what He asks us to do does not make sense.

"Impatience can cause wise people to do foolish things."
—Janette Oke

Sometimes we are impatient. We do not always step out in faith, because we want to know what will happen. We want all of our questions answered. We want to know there will be a "happily ever after" at the "once upon a time." We want to know the rest of the story. We will never have all of the answers. Perhaps we will know everything when we get to heaven. Certain things are revealed to us, however, when we step out in faith and believe. The veil is lifted when we surrender. It is then that understanding comes. God will reveal things to those who have already said yes.

Many people work at the church, take care of others, and do many other good things. Doing those things is good and important. We begrudgingly do many things, however, because we feel responsible, and our hearts are not in it. Where there is no true surrender, there is no breakthrough. We often hold back and do not step fully out into what the Lord has in store for us. We need to grab hold of what has been promised.

It is one thing to possess a promise. It is another thing to be possessed by the promise. To be possessed by a promise means that no matter what happens, our reaction is to respond with the mind of Christ. He wants us to understand because He knows that we struggle and suffer when we do not know what we need to know.

...My people are destroyed from lack of <u>knowledge</u>.
—Hosea 4:6, NIV (emphasis mine)

I worked with a pastor in Ghana who had complete faith in God. His belief in the promises in the Bible possessed him. He knew, without a shadow of a doubt, that the Lord would provide for him. His faith was so strong that he went anywhere the Lord asked him to go, no questions asked.

He told me his story.

I was in Accra ministering to people but I ran out of money. I did not know what to do. I prayed and the Lord told me to go and speak to a man who ran a small transportation company. He was concerned because his busses were not traveling at full capacity, so he was losing money. He asked me to come and pray at the station and ask the Lord to fill the busses. He gave me food to eat and water to drink and five cedi's. I prayed and every bus was full of passengers.

The owner then said, 'You should preach to the people while the busses are being loaded.'

So I started to preach. The next thing I know the Lord is prospering me. People began giving me money. I was very thankful and prayed for the Lord to show me what to do with the money. That night I had a dream and the Lord told me the ingredients for a medicine that could be put on burns, cuts and sores. I bought the ingredients and made the medicine. It works very well. I began selling it. I have made enough money to pay my wife's dowry, and for our wedding. I have also sent all of my brothers through school. Right now, one brother is finishing pharmacy school and he is going to market the medicine for me when he graduates.

I asked, "What is the name of the medicine?"

He said, "Blessed Ointment." Not very original, but it is a fitting name!

This pastor knew how to "stand on the promises of God." We must know and understand what has been promised in scripture. We must completely trust Jesus. If we do not trust Him, we pray and cry out emotionally. We beg and plead with Him to answer our prayers, but deep down we really do not expect Him that He will. We hope He will, but we really do not believe He will. We are not able to access the very thing that Christ has already accomplished for us.

It is like having a bank account that contains everything that we need to live an impactful life. We have legal access to our account, at any time, to withdraw everything that we need: forgiveness, authority, spiritual gifts, provision, and wisdom. We do not redeem anything that we need, however, because we do not really believe our name is on the account. He has given us everything that we need for <u>life and Godliness,</u> but we must be obedient and do what the Lord asks us to do in order to receive it.

> *Grace and peace be yours in abundance through the knowledge of our God and of Jesus our Lord. His divine power has given to us everything that we need for <u>life and godliness</u> through the knowledge of Him who called us by His own glory and goodness. Through these He has given us His very great and <u>precious promises,</u> so that through them you may participate in the divine nature and escape the corruption in the world caused by evil desires.*
> —*2 Peter 1:2-4, NIV (emphasis mine)*

We can stand firmly on the Lord's precious <u>promises</u>. He will direct us in everyday life. The Lord asks us to do something. We have faith that He knows what He is doing and that it is what is best for us. When we are obedient, step out in faith and do what He asks us to do, we can expect something amazing.

"At any moment we can demonstrate our faith by taking action that shows our belief in God's promises!"
—Alisa Hope Wagner

As Helen and I were studying the Bible one day, we talked about the difference between obedience and sacrifice.

She said, "Misty, let me tell you what happened to me one time. I was at the beauty shop sitting under the hair dryer and my heart starts going, *pow, pow, pow*!" Each time she said "pow," she moved her hand up and down over her heart.

She said, "I thought I was having a heart attack. But it was just God."

I laughed with her.

"God said, 'Helen.'" She paused as though this was the most special thing in the world. She smiled and said slowly, "He...knows... my...name!"

He said to me, "I want you to go to South Eastern. Don't stop at your house, although it's on the way."

"What, Lord?" She inquired.

Again the Lord said, "I want you to go straight to the Bible College and tell them you are going to be their piano teacher."

Helen said, "Well I said, 'No!' I was working full time with the symphony. I felt important. I had my own record. I was earning a good salary. Now God was telling me I had to quit playing the piano for the symphony and go teach piano at a small Bible college?! I dug my in heels! I did not want to go! But the Lord had other plans.

"The Lord said, 'Helen!' And my heart began to go pow, pow, pow, pow, like it was coming out of my chest." She motioned to her heart again.

The Lord again said, "Helen."

She interrupted the story, "He had not forgotten my name and He had not forgotten what He had asked me to do. He continued, 'I want you to go straight to the college and tell them that you are going to be their new piano teacher.'" (I loved the way Helen said the word "piano" because she emphasized the "o" at the end as though she was holding a Cheerio in her lips.)

She continued, "Well, I told Him I would go. I finished getting my hair done so I would look nice for the appointment and then went straight there. There was nothing more than a building and a garage there at that time. The school did not even have a music department. I went into the office and a big Swedish woman was standing at the desk. She scared me to death when in a loud, booming voice she asked, 'What do you wish?'"

I can imagine petite Helen looking up at this woman. Helen said, "The woman seemed irritated and I thought, *I don't wish anything. I don't even really understand why I am here.*"

Helen pointed to her head and said, "Satan kept saying, 'Get out of here while you still have the chance!' But that still quiet voice of the Lord said, 'Helen, obey Me.'"

She continued, "So I said to the woman, 'You don't need a piano teacher, do you?'

"Now the woman looked very strange but she said, 'As you wish' and then left the room. She returned almost immediately and said, 'The president of the school wants to see you right away!'

"I went into his office and sat down. He said, 'Ms. Wright, I have a story to tell you. Just last night we had a board of directors' meeting to pray for a classically trained piano teacher. We did not want someone who knew only how to play church music. Not only that, but we also prayed and asked the Lord to send someone that He chose, someone who did not care about how much money they made. We want someone who trusts God to provide for all of their needs.'

"I said, 'I am your new piano teacher.'"

She continued, "I did not tell him but I had not played very much church music and didn't know any hymns. I spent most of my time with classical music. I walked away from a successful career in order to teach piano at a little Bible college that didn't even have a piano. Looking back on it, that was the right thing to do and I am so glad that I did. Can you beat that?"

I said, "No, I can't."

"Faithfulness is not doing something right once but doing something right over and over and over and over."
—Joyce Meyer

Helen taught me that I must be faithful in the little things or God will never trust me with the big things. It proved to be a challenge.

I was in the grocery store shopping one day and noticed someone had left a tube of toothpaste on top of the cans of green beans. The Lord spoke to me and said, "Misty, take the toothpaste back to the toothpaste isle."

I said, "Okay, Lord." I returned the toothpaste to where it belonged.

When I got outside, the store did not have a place to return the shopping carts and they were scattered everywhere. The Lord spoke to me again, "Take your empty cart back into the store." I obeyed and took my shopping cart and other carts that were in the area back into the store.

I could have easily ignored the Lord, but I had promised to be obedient. I refused to be stubborn or lazy. I knew something good would eventually come from it. Revelation comes with surrender. The Lord asked me to do things like that for a while. I wrote an encouraging note as the Lord prompted me. I gave hugs. I cleaned a room that I did not mess up. Most things I did seemed small at first. Those little things led to bigger things.

Some of the things the Lord asks us to do will not always make sense. We may shrug them off or think we have not heard the Lord correctly. We miss a blessing when we do. Helen was right; if we are faithful with the little things, the Lord trusts us with the big things. It is much like our earning the trust of our parents when we are teenagers in order to be given the freedom to do things with our friends.

The Lord does not want to do some things to me or for me, but He wants to do them through me. Amazing things happen. We actually become a part of what God is doing. When the Lord speaks to us, He is putting us in position to implement His will on the earth. The Lord will surprise and bless us if we are obedient.

Indeed the Lord did surprise me one day when Helen and I were together. Helen asked, "Would you like to go to Red Lobster for lunch today?"

I said, "I would love to go, but I used the last money I had putting gas in my car."

She said, "I don't have any money either, but the Lord says it is okay. He'll take care of it."

Now to be totally honest, at that time, my faith was still small. I did, however, have faith that Helen had faith. I believed she really believed that she had heard from the Lord. I believed that she believed that He was going to provide the meal for us. So I hung on to her faith and off we went to the restaurant without a penny in our pockets. We were seated and ordered exactly what we wanted.

After a while the manager, who seemed a little frantic, came to our table. He apologized profusely to us said, "We should have had your food out to you ages ago. I am so sorry! I tell you what; your food is on us! We will pay for everything. Don't you even tip your waiter! Just come back to see us again sometime." Can you beat that?

I was so engrossed in our conversation that I had not even noticed the time. The food was delicious! I am thankful I did not miss that blessing! That experience catapulted my faith into doing the larger things.

I shared that story with someone one time and they accused me of stealing. I did not argue with them. I simply said, "I believe if the Lord has the ability to bless me, He certainly has the ability to prosper the restaurant!" Many years later, I ate at that restaurant again and the service was good, food was excellent and the restaurant was doing well. I paid for the meal this time and was happy to do it!

God will back His Word for any person who will embrace it and who has full intentions to live by it. Helen lived by it! Jesus said, "On earth as it is in heaven."

> *This, then, is how you should pray: Our Father in heaven, hallowed be Your name, Your kingdom come, Your will be done on earth as it is in heaven.*
> —*Matthew 6:9-10, NIV (emphasis mine)*

We should be bringing heaven to earth. The believer pulls on the reality of that world (heaven) until it collides with this one (earth) and this one always gives way. Our assignment is to bring that world into this one. Jesus wants to make Himself known. Jesus does not want us to limit ourselves or limit Him in any way. He made it possible for us to live in victory. Let's look at what Jesus said.

> *I tell you the truth, anyone who has faith in me will do what I have been doing. He will do even greater things than these, because I am going to the father. And I will do whatever you ask in my name, so that the son may bring glory to the father. You may ask me for anything in my name, and I will do it.*
> —*John 14:12-14, NIV (emphasis mine)*

I was in Birmingham, Alabama one day and saw a sign on a church advertising a healing service that evening. The Lord spoke to me and said, "I want you to go to that healing service tonight."

I replied, "Lord, I have never been to a healing service before and have no idea what to expect, but I will go." You see, I had learned from my Red Lobster lesson.

I had a painful ganglion cyst in my wrist and had asked the Lord to heal it. The cyst had grown so large that I could not fully open my hand. I had had a similar cyst surgically removed from my other hand a couple of years earlier. The surgery had been an expensive, painful process. I really did not want to go through that again.

I went into the church that evening and took a seat. The worship team led us in a time of praise and worship. The presence of the Holy Spirit filled the building. The pastor spoke about the sacrifice Jesus made for us by His death on the cross. Believing this makes it possible for us to receive our healing, for by His stripes we are healed.

> *Surely He has borne our griefs and carried our sorrows; Yet we esteemed Him stricken, smitten by God, and afflicted. But He was wounded for our transgressions, He was bruised for our iniquities; the chastisement for our peace was upon Him, and by His stripes we are healed. All we like sheep have gone astray; we have turned, every one, to his own way; and the Lord has laid on Him the iniquity of us all.*
> *—Isaiah 53:4-6, NKJV (emphasis mine)*

The Lord began to give the pastor a word of knowledge about certain people in the congregation. A word of knowledge is simply when the Lord tells us something that we would have no way of knowing. It is a great spiritual gift.

> *But the manifestation of the Spirit is given to each one for the profit of all: for to one is given the word of wisdom through the Spirit, to another the word of knowledge through the same Spirit, to another faith by the same Spirit, to another gifts of healings by the same Spirit, to another the working of miracles, to another prophecy, to another discerning of spirits, to another*

different kinds of tongues, to another the interpretation of tongues.

—1 Corinthians 12:7-10 (emphasis mine)

The pastor walked near where I was sitting and said, "Someone on this side of the church is having trouble with their wrist."

Wow, I was surprised! I stood up and he walked over, took my hand in his hands and began to pray. He said, "Lord Jesus, thank you for healing her wrist. I feel such power flowing here."

At that moment I felt heat like fire flowing through me. I looked at my wrist. The cyst, which was very obvious because it was protruding like a gigantic thumper marble, began to shrink before my very eyes! It completely disappeared and I could feel everything in my hand release and return to normal.

The minister then began to speak a prophetic word over me that has been completely accurate in my life. It was the first prophetic word I had ever received. It was recorded and I play it to remind myself of God's faithfulness. It reminds me that I should never put God in a box and limit Him in any way. I could have been disobedient and not walked into that church. I would have missed my first healing experience. The pastor's obedience in giving me a prophetic word changed my life.

"The ragamuffin who sees his life as a voyage of discovery and runs the risk of failure has a better feel for faithfulness than the timid man who hides behind the law and never finds out who he is at all."
—Brennan Manning, The Ragamuffin Gospel: Good News for the Bedraggled, Beat-Up, and Burnt Out

---

Chapter Thirteen

A Witch, a Robber and a Pee Pot

"When God makes a covenant with us, God says: 'I will love you with an everlasting love. I will be faithful to you, even when you run away from me, reject me, or betray me.' In our society we don't speak much about covenants; we speak about contracts. When we make a contract with a person, we say: 'I will fulfill my part as long as you fulfill yours. When you don't live up to your promises, I no longer have to live up to mine.' Contracts are often broken because the partners are unwilling or unable to be faithful to their terms.

But God didn't make a contract with us; God made a covenant with us, and God wants our relationships with one another to reflect that covenant. That's why marriage, friendship, life in community are all ways to give visibility to God's faithfulness in our lives together."
—Henri J.M. Nouwen, *Bread for the Journey:
A Daybook of Wisdom and Faith*

When I had the divine encounter with God in that little Birmingham church, I stumbled onto the truth. I had heard teaching about healing and read about healing in the Word of God, but I did not fully understand it. We do not have to fully understand something first. Sometimes we will see the fruit of it before we understand it. By obeying the Lord, we learn. Some things we have to experience for ourselves before we "get it."

> *My message and preaching were not with wise and persuasive words, but with demonstration of the Spirit's power, so that your faith may not rest on men's wisdom, but on God's power.*
> — *1 Corinthians 2:4-5, NIV (emphasis mine)*

God is looking for people through whom to show His power. He is looking for those with great character who are willing to be obedient and be used by Him. As we become like Jesus through obedience His presence, His power and His glory are released. When others see God's presence in our lives, they are drawn to what we have. They will be drawn to Christ.

After I experienced my healing miracle, I discovered that my thinking and my beliefs were totally different from most people. Most people believe God for something.

"I'm believing for money."

"I'm believing for a new job."

"I'm believing for healing."

The problem is those types of prayers put all of the pressure and responsibility on the person who prays. If the prayer is not answered in the way the person thinks it should be, he feels the need to explain.

"Maybe I didn't pray right."

"What if I do not have enough faith?"

"I know I didn't do enough."

"Should I have prayed longer?"

"I think I am supposed to just suffer so I can learn from this!"

"The search for a scapegoat is the easiest of all hunting expeditions."

—Dwight D. Eisenhower

We put all of the responsibility for the prayer being answered squarely on our shoulders. Sometimes we will do what Adam and Eve did and try to cast blame. Casting blame is backward thinking and does not line up with God's Word. We should have faith in God. We should trust in the covenant He made with us. We should believe in what Jesus did for us when He went to the cross (Colossians 2:6-7). Strong forward thinking belief puts us in the place of receiving. We do not have to work to make something happen. Faith comes from:

> knowing the truth,
> standing firmly,
> being obedient and
> trusting in who we are in Christ.

The problem is that we do not really know who we are. More than that, we do not really know whose we are.

I am reminded of someone I met in Africa who lived in The Witches' Village. Here is something I wrote in my journal:

The little old woman stands in front of her tiny, round, thatched roof hut. She is holding a short handled, worn down hoe. Her clothing is mismatched, but most of it is colorful. It hangs on her frail body like clothes hang on a scarecrow's crossed broom handles. Her face is etched with years of rejection and struggles. She cannot speak English, but her demeanor is welcoming. She lets me snap a picture. The mud brown hut is in sharp contrast to the green all around. Groundnuts are drying nearby. She is not able to walk very far and so has patches of turned dirt, planted with maize and vegetables, nearby. Every inch of ground has something new growing from it. The rainy season has been good for the village, praise God! It is not easy scratching a living from this ground.

As I look at her, my mind is filled with questions. I wish I could speak her language. How can I believe that this woman with the sad eyes could have ever been a witch? How has she managed to live alone, in exile, here in this witches' village for all of these years? What does it feel like to be rejected by your friends and family? I cannot imagine what she has suffered. Were the accusations made against her false?

What do you do when you are alone and it seems as though the whole world is against you?

I resist the urge to go up and hug her. Ghanaian people do not hug. I decide instead to shake her hand. I smile and give her shoulder a gentle squeeze and invite her to come to the church that is nearby in her village. I can at least give her a mosquito net to sleep under on these hot African nights. It feels like a very small thing, but at least it is something.

Years ago in Ghana, if one was accused of practicing witchcraft or of being a warlock, they were stoned to death. As things became more civilized they would, instead, move them to a village to live. It did not matter if they had not dabbled in casting spells, mixing potions, or sending out curses. A simple accusation would be enough for someone to be ostracized by everyone, thrown out of their village and lose everything, even their identity. Fear is a powerful thing. This woman lost everything. She was no longer a part of her family, or tribe; she was branded as dangerous, and left hopeless, helpless, imprisoned in a village. How would one handle that? What would one do? Can you imagine?

In America we take pride in our heritage and where we live. We research ancestry sites and our family roots. We make sure everything that we do is legal and above reproach so that our inheritance will be passed down to the next generation. Wills are written, covenants made and contracts signed. Everything is tied up in a nice package.

In some ways, however, we have neglected (or are even unaware of) the most important contract or covenant that has ever been transacted on our behalf. We are as lost and helpless as the little old woman in the witches' village. I am talking about the covenant that God made for us and that was ratified by Jesus Christ.

Many people struggle in their relationship with Christ simply because they do not know who they are. In order to walk in faith, we must understand and accept the fact that we are in a covenant agreement with God. God will never break His covenant. He never goes back on what He promised. Some of us, however, are either unaware that we are a part of a covenant or we do not understand how important that covenant is. We cannot access something of which we are not aware. It is like having a key to a safety deposit box that is full of blessings. We will not use the key, however, if we do not know which lock it fits into.

The Bible is a covenant document. A covenant is simply an agreement between two or more parties. It lists the obligations and rewards, as well as what the punishment will be if all or part of the agreement is broken. There are both conditional and unconditional things listed in the agreement. Many times a conditional part of a covenant in the Bible is written as, "If you do this, then you can expect that." God is not a liar and will never go back on His Word. He established His expectations in the very first book of the Bible. He made a covenant with Adam in the Garden of Eden. It is called the Edenic Covenant (Genesis 1:26-28).

God created us in His own image and wants to have a relationship with each of us. He began with Adam and Eve. Mankind became a living life force with a spirit, soul and body. He spoke us into being. In Greek he actually said, "Man be," and that is all that it took.

God then gave us dominion over all of the earth and over all the animals. It is our joint authority with God. God gave man the ability to dominate. It is interesting that we were not given authority over men, however. Yet men strive to gain power over people and dominate them. Look at the dictators, cult leaders and people throughout history who have tried to force their will on others. That is something we were never meant to do. It is not a part of the covenant that God established.

God then said to Adam and Eve, "Be fruitful and increase, fill the earth and subdue it." As a matter of fact, the first sounds heard were words of blessing and then directions of what to do. God blessed us, provided us with everything that we needed and then instructed us. He still does that today. It is important that we learn to listen and then to obey.

Right about now you might be thinking, *Well, that is easier said than done!* You would be right. Look what happened next. Adam and Eve were deceived (Genesis 3). The serpent, Satan, tricked them into disobeying God. It brought every evil, hurtful, destructive thing into their present reality. Adam should have exercised the authority that God had given him and kicked that serpent Satan out of the garden, but he did not. He should have "un-friended him." He had the gift, he had the power, but he did not use them. In time, God put things in motion so that everything would be made right again. He started with a person named Abram. We call this the Abrahamic Covenant and it is very important.

God told Abram to leave his country and his family and go to the land that He would show him. God would bless him and make his name great and make his family into a great nation! He also told Abram that He would bless those who blessed him, and that He would curse those who cursed him. All the families of the earth shall be blessed (Genesis 12:1-3). What a blessing! This is the same blessing given to Adam in the Garden of Eden, but he was disobedient and lost his paradise.

Everywhere Abram went, the blessings followed. There was one condition, however. Abram had to do what God wanted him to do. He asked Abram to move away from home because he was living in a very godless and immoral place. God needed to move him where he and his people could focus on God and on the right things.

Abram was married to Sarai, but they were childless. How was God going to fulfill the promise of making Abram into a great nation if they had no children? The Word of the Lord came to Abram. God said, "I am your shield, your exceeding great reward," (Genesis 15:1). He promised the couple that they would have so many children in fact that their descendants would be "as the stars are in the sky," (Genesis 15:1-5). God reminded him that He would be with him through difficult times and that He would bless him.

God renewed the covenant He had with Abram and with his descendants (Genesis 17:1-9). In it He promised that if Abram would walk blameless before God then He would multiply him exceedingly. He would be the father of many nations and tremendously fruitful. Kings would come from him. God even changed his name from Abram to Abraham, which means, "father of many nations." God would not only honor this covenant with Abraham, but He would also honor it for his descendants. God called it an everlasting covenant. He even went further.

God gave Abraham's wife Sarai the new name Sarah, reminding her she would be the mother of many nations (Genesis 17:15-16). He told her she was to name her son Isaac. He established a covenant with Isaac and with his descendants after him (Genesis 17:19 & 25:11).

That is good news for us, because it means God made an everlasting covenant that included us. It is verified in Romans 4:16 when it says that Abraham is the "<u>father of us all</u>."

> *Therefore, the promise comes by faith, so that it might be by grace and my be guaranteed to all Abraham's off spring - not only to those who are of the law, but also to those who are of the faith of Abraham. He is the <u>father of us all</u>.*
> —*Romans 4:16, NIV (emphasis mine)*

Ultimately, we are all the children of God!

> *He came to that which was His own, but His own did not receive Him. Yet to all who received Him, to those who believe in His name, He gave the right to become <u>children of God</u> – children born not of natural descent, nor of human decision or a husband's will, but born of God*
> —*John 1:11-13, NIV (emphasis mine)*

When God blesses someone, He is conferring upon him the power to increase and prosper in every area of life. The blessing of God made Abraham prosper. He was so rich that he had to separate from his nephew, Lot. Abraham's tribe needed more grazing land. Abraham was so confident in the covenant that he let Lot take the best land in the Jordan valley (Genesis 13:2; 9-11).

Abraham loved God and was obedient; so obedient in fact that he was willing to kill his own son as an offering as God had requested. God stopped him, of course, but honored his faithfulness.

He reaffirmed the covenant with Isaac, promising him everything (Genesis 26:5). Then God proved it to him. A severe famine was in the land and Isaac was taking his people into Egypt because everyone was starving in Gerar. God told Isaac to stay where they were. Isaac planted crops and reaped a hundred fold, because the Lord had blessed him (Genesis 26:12-14).

Little things such as drought or armies or trouble with the economy do not mean much to God. The blessing of Abraham will enable us to prosper no matter what is going on around us. It does not matter what calamity or depression or recession the devil has dreamed up. We are not dependent upon the economy or what the world does. We are depending on the never changing covenant we have with God.

It is ironic that I had recently completed a teaching on covenant with our ministry pastors in Africa before the following story happened. We discussed at length God's provision and protection. This story was taken from my journal.

I was traveling in the Zhong Tong School Bus with ministry staff and seventeen other pastors, four of them, from the neighboring country of Togo. We were on the Tamale' to Yendi road, the last leg of our journey from Kumasi. We had been to the commissioning service for David, our first foreign missionary to Togo. David had put his motorcycle into a canoe he dug out and made by hand and paddled across the river into Togo. He visited villages and planted churches. Now that is serious evangelism! While we were in Kumasi, the Lord had also provided around ten thousand GHC for us to buy drums for our churches that needed them for worship. It had been and wonderfully encouraging day!

We were on a long, barren stretch of road where there was nothing but the African bush. The night was pitch black. There was no moon or stars. The roads were in very poor condition, so trucks and other vehicles broke down all of the time. You got used to going around them when you were driving. So when we came upon a large truck that was pulled over, and another truck stopped in the middle of the road, I didn't think too much about it at first. Then I noticed that cargo and other things had been strewn all over the road. I was thinking, *This doesn't look right.*

In an instant, a man stepped into the beam of our headlights and began coming toward us. He had a large rifle aimed at the bus. A few seconds later, a man holding a 12" serrated hunting knife reached through my open window and held it to my throat. He was yelling at me in the Dogbane language. The pastors all gasped, "Jesus!" at the same time.

My translator Charity stood up, put her fingers to her lips and said, "SShhhhh, don't say a word." She then led the way, got off of the bus and lay face down on the ground. The others followed suit. The men roughly pushed everyone to the ground, and thoroughly searched each one of us as we lay in the dirt. They took our phones and everything we had in our pockets.

The passengers of regular transport buses paid the drivers for the trip. It was not unusual for the drivers to carry money. These men did not understand that we were all missionaries traveling on our ministry bus. They assumed that we were paying passengers. Our driver was on the ground near Charity. They took what little money that he had, but were not satisfied so they started kicking and beating him.

One man grabbed Charity by her shoulder and rolled her over. He lifted her slightly off of the ground by her collar and stared intently at her face. He then pushed her back down on the ground. I learned later that Charity had seen his face and he was looking to see if he knew who she was. If a victim recognizes a thief, the thief has been known to kill them. The pastors knew this and deliberately would not look their captors in the face. Thankfully, Charity was spared.

There were two children on the bus with us: a three-year-old little boy and a three-month-old baby. One of the robbers insisted that the mother had hidden money in the baby's diaper, so he grabbed the baby and ripped her diaper off. The baby began crying. As soon as the robber moved on to search someone else, the mother sat up and began nursing the child so she would stop crying.

As I was lying down I noticed the flashing lights of a police car off in the distance. In a normal voice I said, "The police are coming."

I did not know if the robbers spoke English, but I knew some our pastors did. I was hoping it would encourage them. If the robbers knew the police were coming, perhaps they would become afraid and run. We were miles from the nearest village and probably two hours from a police station. Where in the world did the police come from? How did they know anyone was in danger?

By now, some of the robbers were on the bus going through everyone's things. The man who had put the knife at my throat was looking around the floorboard where I had been sitting.

Within three or four minutes the police arrived on the other side of the blockade where vehicles had been stopped. The moment the robbers saw the lights of the police car, some of them ran into the bush.

Two gunshots rang out.

We all kept our heads down, concerned the police might mistake us for the robbers.

John was a policeman from Yendi, and was actually a part of our ministry. He happened to be the first one on the scene. It is just like the Lord to send someone that we knew to be our rescuer. He had a gun in one hand and a flashlight in the other.

He asked in English, "Is anyone hurt or injured?"

We said, "We are all right." Our driver was bloody, scraped and bruised, but able to get up and drive the bus.

When everyone realized the police officer was John, we were relieved. Almost at one time everyone began to get up and to pray out loud, thanking Jesus.

"Thank you, Jesus, for our lives!"

"Thank you Jesus for your protection!"

"Thank you Father!"

"Praise your faithfulness!"

John told us to get back on the bus. We complied as quickly as we could.

He asked, "Where did they go?" We pointed in the direction of the bush in which they ran.

We heard more gunshots.

I was about to sit down in my seat and realized the robber had left the knife he had put in my face right there on the seat.

The moment that everyone was on the bus, our driver started the engine and began to move forward. When our headlights came on we could see that other vehicles, including one of the large trucks, began to do the same.

Several people who had been lying on the ground in front of the trucks began to move a large tree and other things that the robbers had used to block the road.

As our headlights passed by, I noticed a man who was leaning over his motorcycle and holding his head. Blood ran down his face.

The Lord protected us. My wallet and flashlight were stolen. They did not have time to open my backpack, which was in plain view. I was thankful I had fussed about putting on my shoes because the robber, thinking I had hidden something there, opened the bag that I had used to hold water and bread. It had been sitting at my feet and next to my shoes. My laptop computer and cameras were in my backpack and in plain sight. My laptop was my lifeline to my family and friends and I would have hated to lose it. Thankfully I had turned my passport in to the visa office so I could get an extension in order to stay in the country. I lost some money and my immunization records, driver's license, etc. All are trivial things if you really think about it.

The Lord really blessed us. John told me later that this sort of thing rarely happens. These robbers will go through everyone possessions and if they do not get enough money, they will beat the men badly (especially the person driving) and usually rape the women. If you talk back to them, they will beat you. They have even been known to kill people. They are brutal. It is no wonder everyone began praising Jesus and singing. Thank you, Jesus!

When the police arrived, two of the robbers lay down on the ground and pretended to be victims. They were arrested. Two more stole motorcycles that were there and tried to escape. They were eventually apprehended. We hope that these four who were caught might aide in the arrest of others. They came from a group of people who live by moving cattle from place to place.

I found out later that everyone was concerned for my safety because they knew that I did not know that people did things like this. They were afraid that if I said anything to them that they would hurt me.

I asked Charity how she calmly knew what to do. She said that the same thing had happened to her mother several years ago. Her mother told her, "If this ever happens to you, do not argue, just do what they ask and give them what you have." Charity's sister was in the hospital and her mom went to sell some things and get the money and medicine she needed to take care of her daughter at the hospital. While traveling back to the hospital, robbers did the same thing to her. She gave them all of her money without a word, so they left her alone. The driver in her case was shot in the leg and eventually lost the leg up to the upper thigh.

Her mother went back and sold everything they had to get more money to pay the hospital bill. The sad part of the story is that Charity's sister died in the hospital. Her mother has lived with regret. Because of what those robbers had done, she was not able to get the money to the hospital soon enough. In Ghana, the doctors will not treat you unless you can pay for the medicine and services ahead of time. She did not get to spend the time with her daughter that she needed and wanted to at the end of her life.

Pastor Mark, a ministry leader, was on the bus with us. I asked him, "Has this sort of thing had happened to you before?"

He said, "Yes, only the last time, they did not get my money or phone."

"What did you do?" I enquired.

He said, "There was a hole in my seat, so I put the money in the hole. I put my cell phone inside my sock. When they searched me and asked me where my money was, I lied, 'Your brother already took my money.'

"They believed you?" I asked.

He said, "Yes, and they left me alone."

Curious, I asked him, "How did that make you feel?"

Mark said, "It is just a part of being in the ministry. Paul suffered, too. He was shipwrecked, and put into prison. It is an honor to experience these things for the cause of Jesus Christ. We are to be like Paul."

As I was alone and trying to process what had happened, the Lord gave me this verse: *"Surely the arm of the Lord is not too short to save, nor his ear too dull to hear," Isaiah 59:1.*

God confirms the covenant all through the generations (Genesis 41). Abraham's great grandson Joseph started out as a slave in the ungodly nation of Egypt. He found favor everywhere he went and everything he touched prospered. He became the second most powerful person, next to Pharaoh, and saved his family and the nation from starvation. The entire country was blessed because of Joseph's covenant with God. Joseph believed; Joseph received. Every person that proclaimed, "The covenant is for me!" prospered, even in the middle of difficult times.

We are heirs of even more than what Joseph was promised in his covenant. God has provided not only the natural blessings that Abraham, Isaac and Joseph enjoyed, but also every spiritual blessing that Jesus won for us when He died on the cross and rose again! God promised Abraham, "Thy seed shall possess the gates of His enemies," (Genesis 22:17). That is exactly what happened. Jesus, Abraham's seed and heir to the Abrahamic covenant, died, went into Satan's domain and defeated him. He came out with the keys of death and hell!

I am the living one; I was dead, and behold I am alive forever and ever! And I hold the <u>keys of Hades and of Death</u>.
                            —Revelations 1:18, NIV (emphasis mine)

We have everything that was promised to us in the old covenant, plus the fulfillment of the promise of the Spirit. The moment we gave our lives to Christ, we were born again and have the Holy Spirit dwelling inside of us! We can be <u>forgiven</u>!

We have inherited it all! We are anchored!

This is the covenant that I will make with the house of Israel after that time, declares the Lord. <u>I will put my laws in their minds and write them on their hearts</u>. I will be their God, and they will be My people. No longer will a man teach his neighbor, or a man his brother, saying, 'Know the Lord,' because they will all know me, from the least of them to the greatest. For I will forgive their wickedness and remember <u>their sins no more</u>.
                          —Hebrews 8:10-13, NIV (emphasis mine)

God backed it with an oath. God took an oath, swearing by Himself, because there is no one greater and it is impossible for Him to lie. He promised to honor the same covenant made with Abraham, Isaac, Jacob and the generations that followed. God made a covenant with Moses we call the Mosaic Covenant (Exodus 24:19-24). It was conditional (Exodus 19:5-8) and God reminded the people of their obligation to be obedient. It was the law until Christ came.

God continued the covenant with David, the Davidic Covenant (2 Samuel 7; 1 Chronicles 17:11-14; 2 Chronicles 6:16), and reaffirmed the earlier covenants made with Abraham and Moses. Two unconditional parts of this covenant are that God would establish David's bloodline forever, and give them a home so they would not be oppressed (2 Samuel 7:10). His son Solomon would build a house of worship in God's name (2 Samuel 7:12-13) and the Messiah would come through David's bloodline.

The Messiah Jesus Christ came and because of what He did, we have been given spiritual authority and blessings. Jesus said that if we believe in Him, and in the things that He did, we will do even greater things. He followed by saying <u>whatever we ask</u> in His Name, <u>He will do</u> so that the Father will be glorified through us.

> *I tell you the truth, anyone who has faith in me will do what I have been doing. He will <u>do even greater things</u> than these, because I am going to the Father. And <u>I will do whatever you ask in my name</u>, so that the Son may bring glory to the Father. You may ask me for anything in my name, and I will do it*
>   *—John 14:12-13, NIV (emphasis mine)*

Look at the covenant between God and Jesus concerning us:
This covenant is eternal (Hebrews 13:20).
Christ is a Deity who lived in an earthly body (Colossians 2:9).
The way to heaven is to believe in Jesus Christ (John 6:25-58).
Jesus was given authority over all people (Matthew 28:18).
Those who believe in him will have eternal life (John 3:15-17).
Everything that Jesus did came from His Father (John 8:28-29).
We are protected by the power of Jesus' Name (Acts 3:6).
We are sanctified by the truth of the Word of God (John 17:19).
Jesus makes God known to us so that the love of God will be in us (John 17).
Christ is sitting at the right hand of God (Mark 16 & Luke 22).
Christ is the mediator between God and mankind (1 Timothy 2:5).
God put Jesus in charge of everything (Hebrews 2:6-15).
Jesus became the atoning sacrifice for our sin (1 John 1-2).
We are healed by the blood of Jesus (1 Peter 2:24).
Jesus is the good shepherd, and He knows His sheep (John 10:1-5).
Jesus knows each one of us and we can know Him (John 10:14-15).
Jesus redeemed us so we are now no longer bondage slaves (Galatians 3:13-14).
We are now God's children (Galatians 4:1-7).
We are made righteous because of the righteous act of Jesus (Romans 5:18).
We should live for Christ (2 Corinthians 5:14).

It is God's desire to convince us beyond a shadow of doubt that we are His heirs.

When Jesus Christ was crucified, He fulfilled the covenant and broke the <u>curse</u> that came upon us when Adam and Eve transgressed in the garden.

Christ has redeemed us from the <u>curse</u> of the law, having become a curse for us, for it is written: 'Cursed is everyone who is hung on a tree', that the blessing given to Abraham might come upon the gentiles in Christ Jesus, that we might receive the promise of the Spirit through faith.
—Galatians 3:13, NKJV (emphasis mine)

We are the Gentiles! We are the <u>heirs of the world</u>!

It was not through law that Abraham and his offspring received the promise that he would be <u>heir of the world</u>, but through the righteousness that comes by faith.
—Romans 4:13, NIV (emphasis mine)

We have received everything through righteousness that comes by faith. Everything is there for us if we will just believe!

Faith opens the door. Satan tries to talk us out of our inheritance. He does not have an inheritance of his own. He has to steal everything that he gets from the seed of Abraham, because the whole world belongs to us. We should not let the devil push us around! That promise, that oath, should rise up within us: "I am an heir and have inherited a promise. God will bless me! I will be a blessing! I will succeed! I rebuke unbelief! Satan, you get out of here because you will not steal my inheritance! In Jesus' Name, amen!"

When we are faced with things in our lives that seem overwhelming, we need to remind ourselves of who we are and what has been given to us. What seems impossible for us is, to God, a miracle waiting to happen.

"Abraham, you are old and Sarah's womb is dead, why don't you have a child?"

"Okay."

"Abraham, four armies have taken your relatives and everything they own, gather your little flock of people and go and get them."

"Sure, why not?"

"Isaac, there is a famine everywhere. The ground is dry and there is no water. Plant seeds and grow a crop."

"How big of a crop do you want me to plant?"

"Misty, Jesus went to the cross for you. He can heal your wrist with the snap of His fingers! Go to the healing service. Receive!"

"Absolutely!"

In every instance they believed, no matter how outrageous it sounded to them. They did exactly as they were directed. Miracles happened and the whole world sat up and noticed.

We are like a prince or princess who lives in a castle. What is our responsibility? To do what our father, the king, tells us to do. We should see ourselves as a child of the King, with all of the benefits and privileges that come with it. The trouble is most of us do not really know who we are. We do not see ourselves as royalty. We see ourselves as the chambermaid who is responsible for cleaning the bedroom and pouring out the pee pots. We act like slaves instead, always begging and never expecting very much.

We must change the way we see ourselves or we will never expect very much from God. We are sons and daughters of the Most High King. We are His children and He really wants to bless us and be involved in our lives. Our Father knows what is best for us and will work with us so that our lives are extraordinary. God will open doors of opportunity that we cannot even imagine.

Each morning when I commit my day to the Lord I pray for divine appointments, opened doors of opportunity and miracles. Then I spend the rest of the day watching to see what the Lord is going to do. I talk with the Lord about my needs, hopes and dreams, and then wait expectantly for Him to move. I am obedient and do what He tells me to do when He tells me to do it. It is exciting and keeps my mind on Him.

I live each day with expectation; not because I deserve anything from Him, because I do not. It is not about that. My expectations are high because I know that I am His child. I know how He feels about me. I know what I mean to Him. I am hopelessly, completely in love with Him and He knows it. I am in a relationship with Him and learn more each day about His character, nature and personality.

I know that I am His princess, His little girl. He still disciplines me at times and that is good. A good Father will do what is best for His child. He knows me better than I know myself. He is wise. I trust Him completely. Satan does not want us to love like that. Satan does not want us to trust like that. What would happen if every Christian gave themselves completely over to the amazing things our Father has in store for us? Oh, how we might change the world if we would only trust Him and really let Him love us. How great our lives would be if we let Him bless us and if we opened our hearts to receive. I would like to live in that kind of world.

"True faith means holding nothing back. It means putting every hope in God's fidelity to His Promises."
—Francis Chan,
Crazy Love: Overwhelmed by a Relentless God

Chapter Fourteen

A Clavichord, an Angel and a Guinea Fowl

"When God is our Holy Father, sovereignty, holiness, omniscience, and immutability do not terrify us; they leave us full of awe and gratitude. Sovereignty is only tyrannical if it is unbounded by goodness; holiness is only terrifying if it is untempered by grace; omniscience is only taunting if it is unaccompanied by mercy; and immutability is only torturous if there is no guarantee of goodwill."

—Ravi Zacharias

I was driving to the church where I worked early on a Sunday morning. There is normally little traffic on the road during that time. As I was turning in an intersection, a speeding car ran the red light and slammed into the side of my car, hitting just in front of the right rear tire. At that moment everything went into slow motion. My car spun in circles, lifted off the ground. The seatbelt tightened, my Bible flew around inside the car, and broken glass slid everywhere. The airbag deployed and my head hit something. There was a strong smell of gasoline as my car settled in the bushes of the median. I saw the astonished faces of the other drivers. Everything happened in an instant.

As you might imagine, I went through a range of emotions in a very short time. What happened? I am alive! Praise God! Is the other driver all right? Is my car ruined? The entire rear end was hanging off. I knew my car would have to be totaled. I began to get angry. The car had been an answer to prayer. It was a gift from God to me and now it was gone. I could feel the anger rising up within me. It was reasonable to be angry, but anger is not healthy. I do not get overly emotional in emergencies. In fact, the exact opposite happens; I become calm, rational, and even deliberate.

The police, fire truck and paramedics were there quickly. The man who hit me got out of his car, which was badly damaged, and was escorted to the police car. He seemed unhurt except that his lip was bleeding. I knew the best way to deal with my anger was to forgive the driver. I walked over, before they handcuffed him, stuck out my hand and told him my name. He pulled back. Trembling, he told me his name and shook my hand. I forgave him.

I learned from the arresting officer that the driver spoke no English, had no driver's license and was in the country illegally.

Although I was badly shaken, I went to work. Not my best decision. I arrived in time for children's church and began with our usual time of prayer. That morning, however, when I opened my mouth to pray my words came out jumbled. I knew what I wanted to say, but could not say it. My headache was becoming unbearable. A friend drove me to the emergency room. After seeing an assortment of doctors and specialists and being put through a battery of tests, I was diagnosed with a brain injury. I lost my short-term memory and ability to speak. I had to write everything down on paper to remember.

I was instructed by the doctors to go home and do absolutely nothing for at least six months. They said, "Do not cook, do not clean, do absolutely nothing, which means absolutely nothing." I could not read or watch television. Six months! I was responsible for a growing, thriving children's ministry. People depended upon me, how could I be away for six months?

I was, however, obedient. It would have been easy to feel sorry for myself and become depressed. That would make things worse. I decided to put my hope in God and to believe in His Word. In my mind I prayed, "Lord, thank you for the treatment and diagnosis of the doctors. I appreciate what they have done for me, but I do not come into agreement with them. They are not the last word: You are. The Bible says You were tortured and crucified. It is by those stripes that I am healed. Lord Jesus, I receive my healing. I will do whatever the doctors have told me to do until You tell me what I need to do. I trust You, Lord. Thank You for my complete and total healing, in Jesus' Name, amen." (See 1 Peter 2:24.) A sense of peace settled in my heart and spirit.

Six weeks later I was still home doing nothing. The doctors were correct. Anything that I tried to do made my excruciating headache feel worse. Nothing had improved. I prayed in the spirit. The only time I spoke properly was when I prayed out loud in tongues, knowing that praying in tongues has nothing to do with the mind; it comes from the Spirit. There was no shudder or hesitation in my words. It was as though nothing was wrong with me.

One morning while praying the Lord spoke to me and told me to go to the Woodlawn United Methodist Church Women's Retreat in Destin, Florida. I did not want to go to the women's retreat. The medication had addled me, I could not speak, and I still had no short-term memory. The tremendous pain in my head was indescribable. I knew people would surround me to talk about the accident. They would ask questions that I could not answer. I would not remember to whom I spoke. Oh, it would be awful!

However, I had learned the importance of being obedient when the Lord asked something of me. If I wanted to be healed, I knew I had to go to the retreat. The Lord told me my friend Vivian was coming to visit me, so I wrote it down. When she arrived with food, I smiled and then wrote a note and asked her if she would take me to the retreat. "Are you serious?" she said. I was going to give the Lord an opportunity to bring His world into my world.

After the first session on that Friday night, I approached the speaker, Janice Spencer, and communicated the best that I could what had happened to me. I believed that if she anointed me with oil, laid hands on me and prayed for me I would be healed. She and other Holy Spirit filled intercessors prayed for me. It was a very simple prayer. As soon as she said, "Amen," my excruciating headache simply disappeared. I opened my mouth to thank them and the words tumbled out correctly.

Janice said, "Do you realize you are talking correctly? We can understand every word you are saying!"

It was an amazing experience! I did not see angels or hear the "Hallelujah Chorus." It happened very simply. The pain was gone and I could speak. I was not sure about my short-term memory, however. I went to my hotel room, opened my Bible and began to read healing scriptures. It was the first time I had been able to read the Bible out loud in six weeks. I read for about forty-five minutes and then proclaimed, "It is done, in Jesus' Name." I slept through the night. The next morning I spoke to everyone during breakfast and the ladies were floored! They had seen my pitiful condition the night before. They were astounded! It was a miracle! Praise Jesus! Word spread quickly and on Sunday morning at church everyone was all a buzz about the miracle that happened at the women's retreat.

It is interesting that this is not the first time someone had prayed for me during the six weeks I was injured. I do not know why the Lord chose to bring healing at the retreat. Maybe it is because it was a living testimony, not just a story they heard about. I was one of which they had actually been a part. Whatever the reason, I am very thankful for the healing and that I was obedient and did what the Lord told me to do. Oh, how different things might have been if I had not been obedient.

"Miracles are a retelling in small letters of the very same story which is written across the whole world in letters too large for some of us to see."

—C.S. Lewis

I was a little surprised at some reactions towards my healing. One man said with a very angry tone, "I am glad God healed you," then he shrugged his shoulders and huffed off.

A lady said, "God must really love you." Was she implying that He did not love her?

Another man said, "Well, you work for the church." I wanted to tell him that my work had absolutely nothing to do with my healing—healing is freely given to everyone—but he did not seem to want to listen. So I got on my face before the Lord to talk with Him about these things.

"The greatness of the man's power is the measure of his surrender."

—William Booth

Someone asked me how I encouraged myself during the time before I was healed. What did I think about? Those are excellent questions. I told them that anytime an ungodly mindset started to rear its ugly head, I came into agreement with the truth from the Word of God. I thanked the Lord that I was already healed. Let me explain.

There was no denying that I had the injury. It was a painful, debilitating experience. I did not deny feeling badly and I did not pretend everything was all right. I did not give into my feelings, curl up and feel sorry for myself. Yes, it was a fact that I was injured, but the truth is healing is in the atonement (Romans 5). The truth is that it is by His stripes (wounds) that I have already been healed.

He himself bore our sins in his body on the cross, so that we might die to sins and live for righteousness; by his wounds you have been healed.
—1 Peter 2:24, NIV (emphasis mine)

Truth trumps fact. Facts can change; truth never changes. I chose to believe the truth. I imagined a whip, a cat of nine tails, tearing through the flesh of Jesus. I pictured His blood pouring from Him and covering the ground. It is because of His suffering that I already have my healing. I believed and I received. I did not try to conjure up faith. As a matter of fact, my expectation was so strong that it absorbed all of my attention. I was excited about the healing I was about to experience. What would it be like? How was it going to happen? I looked forward to it! I knew

I was going to be healed. I felt it deep inside. That knowing was more real to me than anything tangible.

Prayer means believing He <u>will</u> do something. Praise means believing that He <u>has</u> done something. I praised God for my healing before I received my healing. I praised God through it all.

If I question whether something is the will of God while I am praying for it, then I will have no faith! I must first know His will. If we doubt God's intentions, we will actually turn away from God's blessings. When it comes to receiving healing, Jesus is the standard. He healed all those who were sick. He did not leave one person and say, "I'm going to let you stay sick because I am building character in you." No!

He did not say, "I am so sorry that I cannot heal you because you do not have enough faith." No!

He never said, "Come on, everyone. I could heal this person, but someone in this room does not really believe." No!

Jesus loves, period! He paid an awful price because He loves us so much. Jesus never caused people to be sick (Luke 4:40 & Matthew 14:14). If we, as the body of Christ, are beaten up and broken, sick and infirm, we will not be able to bring about change in this world. Those who are not saved should see Christ in us. Our experiences with Jesus should draw others to us and to Him. They should look at us and say, "I want what they have."

I looked at my friend Helen's life and said, "Lord, I want what she has!"

"Miracles are like pimples, because once you start looking for them you find more than you ever dreamed you'd see."

—Lemony Snicket, *The Lump of Coal*

"Sovereign" means supreme ruler, someone superior in power and authority. Perhaps a better way of saying it: God is in control. Absolutely nothing that happens in the universe is outside of God's influence and authority. Consider a few of the claims the Bible makes about God: God is above all things and before all things. He is the alpha and the omega, the beginning and the end (Revelations 21:6). He is immortal, and He is present everywhere. Everyone can know Him.

God created all things and holds all things together, both in heaven and on earth, both visible and invisible (Colossians 1:16).

God knows all things past, present, and future. There is no limit to His knowledge, for God knows everything completely, even before it happens (Romans 11:33).

God can do all things and accomplish all things. Nothing is impossible for Him (Jeremiah 32:17).

God is in control of all things and rules over all things. He has power and authority over nature, earthly kings, history, angels, and demons. Even Satan himself has to ask God's permission before he can act (Psalm 103).

Because he is sovereign, He is the ultimate source of all power, and authority. It is God's sovereignty that makes Him superior to all other gods and makes Him, and Him alone, worthy of worship. God loves us and wants the best for us.

And we know that in all things God works for the good of those who love Him, who have been called according to His purpose.
—Romans 8:28, NIV (emphasis mine)

For years Helen had a clavichord in her apartment at Redmont Gardens because it played softly and would not disturb her neighbors. It was not until she moved to the Fair Haven Retirement Community that she was able to play the piano again. There was a beautiful grand piano downstairs in the central gathering area. It was a large room with a wide balcony.

The activity director of the retirement community asked Helen if she would play the piano for the residents. Helen talked to the Lord about it. "Lord, may I play for the residents who live here?"

He said, "Not yet. You need to prepare. Go and get the hymnbook and I will show you which songs to play. Write down the words to each hymn. Then write down scripture that applies to those hymns." It took some time, but Helen obeyed.

159

Curious, Helen asked, "Lord, why do I need to write down the words to the hymns?"

The Lord said, "If you want the living water to flow out of you, wisdom and understanding need to be in you."

I was there to hear her play one time. Helen sat down at the piano and began to play. The beautiful music floated down the hallways. One by one doors opened and the residents began gathering. Chairs were filled and people in wheelchairs and on walkers lined the walls. A weighty presence of the Holy Spirit fell on the place. I was so overwhelmed with love that I began to cry. I looked around and noticed I was not the only one. Even some of the men took their handkerchiefs from their pockets. It was one of the most moving things I have ever experienced. We were all mesmerized. I heard stories about how the presence of the Holy Spirit had healed people while listening to Helen play. I knew that this was true.

When Helen had played the last hymn she asked, "Lord, would you like for me to play some more?"

He said, "No, Helen. That is enough."

God loves us! God will make <u>good</u> things happen in our lives! He has the power and authority to back up that promise! He is the only one who can! Nothing comes into our lives that God does not allow.

Some of us are dealing with really crummy and difficult things in life. It is easy to get discouraged and let our faith in God slip. We look at our circumstances and think there is nothing good in this. I have felt this way before and encouraged myself by studying the life of Moses. This man had serious challenges!

Moses was the leader of a large group of grumblers and complainers who were enslaved to Pharaoh. His people had suffered for years and Moses did not know what to do; not to mention, Moses was a wanted man and could be arrested at any time. The glory of God came and He spoke to Moses through a burning bush. He must have really needed encouraging. Who wouldn't take a burning bush seriously? Power came in that burning bush. This fire of God empowered Moses to challenge Pharaoh, "Pharaoh, let my people go!" This power changed Pharaoh's circumstances until he humbled himself and stepped aside (Exodus 1-14).

The same problem solving power that was in the burning bush is available to us. God wants us to stand before our pharaohs. He wants us to pray hard for, and expect to have, the same favor that God bestowed upon Moses to be given to us. God partners with us and will move problems, obstacles and mountains out of our way, just as He did for Moses. We can pray our way through. We can even pray and get ahead of a problem before it happens.

Satan will try to steal, kill and destroy but there is hope because sometimes God, in His mercy, intervenes. My nephew Jordan was driving one night down an unlit country road in his red Ford Ranger pick-up truck. He was going around a curve when his front right tire ran off of the road. He immediately jerked the steering wheel to the left and over compensated. The truck tire caught on the pavement and began flipping engine over tailgate. The truck landed on its tires on the opposite side of the road facing in the opposite direction.

When my sister Stormy arrived on the scene she saw a twisted wreck of a truck. Jordan was holding a tee shirt to his face where he had a small scratch that was bleeding. When she asked what happened he said, "Mom, you are not going to believe it! When the truck started flipping I felt something hold me to the seat. My head, shoulders and legs did not move! Something pulled my feet under me, my arms down to my side and my back to the seat. It had to be an angel!" The paramedics arrived and asked where the victim was. Jordan said, "I was driving." They looked at the truck, looked at him and shook their heads.

The paramedics were amazed because his blood pressure was not even elevated. The truck had rolled several times, and all of the windows had shattered. The cab of the truck was caved in, except where Jordan was sitting. Jordan is 6' 5" and sitting in a small truck and did not even bump his head. The airbag had deployed, yet left no marks or bruises. He was not even bruised from the seat belt.

Later when I talked to Jordan about the accident he said, "Misty, I know that God has something in mind for my life, because I should be dead." We do not understand why God allowed this to happen. Jordan hated to lose his truck, but the experience left him feeling optimistic about his future. Stormy and I have been praying hard for Jordan since he was conceived. God honors our prayers.

We do not have a problem with the sovereignty of God when it comes to the big things; after all, He created the moon and the stars. We can go with that. They are far away from us and we have nothing to do with the stars, anyway. *God, you take care of the fish and the birds, and all of the animals, too. Thanks, God!*

Nevertheless, we have a problem when it becomes more personal. To say that God is in charge of all that happens to us—the good and the bad, the happy and the sad, the positive and the negative—gives us pause. To believe that He knows what is best for us and that he will work out the detailed plans in our everyday lives; well, that is another story. When there is trouble, we want to know who is running the show. If the man in charge is not running the show, pray tell, who is? That is what sovereignty is all about. It answers the question, "Who is running the show?" A great deal is at stake in the answer to that question.

> *The Lord has established his throne in heaven, and his kingdom rules over all.*
> —*Psalm 103:19, NIV (emphasis mine)*

Yes, God rules over everything, but He limited Himself through the covenant He has with us. Three wills greatly affect us. There is man's will, the will of God and Satan's will.

We have been given the wonderful gift of choice. God does not make us love and obey Him; we must choose to love and obey Him. If He made us obey, we would be nothing more than slaves. God wants a relationship with each of us and there must be freedom and trust in that relationship. Like a good father, He trusts us to be responsible. He gives us everything that we need to live a victorious life. Because He wants a relationship with us, He communicates through the Holy Spirit who lives inside of us and is our Helper. We have the Word of God that is alive and powerful. We can ask for amazing spiritual gifts! We have been given His body of people, the church, to which we can turn.

If we deliberately sin, make choices that destroy our world, or disregard the Word of God, He will not go against our free will. He will let us live with the consequences of that sin. This breaks His heart, but we are accountable for our actions.

162

Many Christians misunderstand the will of God by believing that, because God is omnipotent and omniscient, His will is always done. It is quite clear from Scriptures that God's will is not always done and, in fact, it is not normally done. It is not His will that anyone perish, but people step over Jesus Christ on their way to hell every day! Although God is omnipotent, He limited Himself through conditional covenant with His creation, man. Therefore, He cannot always do His will. God cannot lie. When He says, "If you do this, then I will do that," He is limited by His words – His covenant. In fact, that is the key factor that Satan uses to attack Christians. He knows God cannot act contrary to His Word.

If we do not know what the will of God is, we will use God's Sovereignty as an excuse. We conveniently blame things on God. If we believe everything is His fault, then we do not have to take personal responsibility. After all, God is sovereign. He must have determined that a car accident causing a brain injury would be just what I needed to make me a better person. Oh, and my ministry is not important. Others will have to step up and do the work. If God willed it, then I guess I will have to live with it. Wrong! That is not God's character or nature!

There is the <u>will of Satan</u>. Satan's job description is to kill, steal, deceive and destroy. Satan's will is completely opposed to God's will. God is light. Satan is darkness. God is truth. Satan is a liar (John 8:44). God is life. Satan brings death.

Satan is angry. He was kicked out of heaven. Satan committed the first sin. He incited the first rebellion. He devised the temptation in the Garden of Eden. He knows He will endure a miserable, agonizing eternity. He cannot hurt God, so he <u>hurts</u> what matters most to God— His children. Peace and harmony reigned before Satan deceived Adam and Eve.

Be self-controlled and alert. Your enemy the <u>devil prowls around</u> like a roaring lion <u>looking for someone to devour</u>.
—1 Peter 5:8, NIV (emphasis mine)

Satan stirs up trouble. He makes false accusations. He incites us to commit evil deeds. He is a world-wrecker and a home-destroyer. "The thief comes only to <u>steal</u> and <u>kill</u> and <u>destroy</u>."

Jesus said, The thief comes only to <u>steal</u> and <u>kill</u> and <u>destroy</u>; I have come that they may have life, and have it to the full.
— *John 10:10, NIV (emphasis mine)*

When Helen was a young woman, she fell in love with someone who played in the symphony along with her. They had a romantic courtship, which included Bible study and church. When they got married, however, he refused to go to church and to read the Bible anymore. Helen became pregnant and he became angry. He did not want her to have the baby. When it was time for her to deliver, he did not even go to the hospital to be with her during the birth. She was heartbroken.

She had a normal delivery and the nurse took the baby to clean. Suddenly, she heard a loud thud. Helen said. "The nurses gasped! It felt as like the air was sucked out of the room. I knew my baby was dead. The nurse who was carrying my baby had dropped it on its head."

Helen said, "Not long afterwards, my husband quietly divorced me." Her world came crashing down upon her. She lost her baby and her husband at the same time. She was a divorced woman during a time when "divorce" was a dirty word. Helen felt very alone and went into a deep depression. In anguish, she cried out to God. He lovingly answered her and gave her a promise that turned her life around.

Sing, barren woman, you who never bore a child; burst into song, shout for joy, you who were never in labor; because more are the children of the desolate woman than of her who has a husband, says the Lord. Enlarge the place of your tent, stretch your tent curtains wide, do not hold back; lengthen your cords, strengthen your stakes. For you will spread out to the right and to the left; your descendants will dispossess nations and settle in their desolate cities. Do not be afraid; you will not be put to shame. Do not fear disgrace; you will not be humiliated. You will forget the shame of your youth and remember no more the reproach of your widowhood.

For your Maker is your husband—the Lord Almighty is his name- the Holy One of Israel is your Redeemer; he is called the God of all the earth. The Lord will call you back as if you were

a wife deserted and distressed in spirit- a wife who married young, only to be rejected, says your God. For a brief moment I abandoned you, but with deep compassion I will bring you back. In a surge of anger I hid my face from you for moment, but with everlasting kindness I will have compassion on you, says the Lord your Redeemer.
—Isaiah 54:1-8 (emphasis mine)

Helen believed that she would have many spiritual children. A promise God fulfilled! Stormy and I are just two of her many spiritual children.

Satan comes to steal our purity, our honesty, our integrity, our decency, our kindness, our compassion, our generosity, our faith, and all godly impulse. He intends to destroy our friendships, our homes, our careers, and our godly ambitions. He will rip apart our marriages and our families. He has taken dead aim at our churches, too. He wants to stir up controversy, hatred, division, strife and quarreling. He wants churches split, and to leave pastors defeated. He manipulates situations so Christians become bitter and friendships shatter. He works to remain the "god of this age."

And even if our gospel is veiled, it is veiled to those who are perishing. The god of this age has blinded the minds of unbelievers, so that they cannot see the light of the gospel of the glory of Christ, who is the image of God.
—2 Corinthians 4:3-4, NIV (emphasis mine)

We know that we are children of God, and that the whole world is under the control of the evil one.
—1 John 5:19 (emphasis mine)

We must fight back through prayer, through spiritual warfare. Many people are not comfortable praying. We must learn how to put on spiritual armor and how to use the Word of God as a weapon (Ephesians 6:10-18). People shrink back at the thought of taking authority over Satan and his demons. Most of us walk into battle each day with our little pocketknives when Satan is armed with bombs and machine guns.

165

We blame God for what Satan is doing. We blame God when we should be taking authority over things ourselves. Are we more afraid of Satan than we are of God?

We want to ignore Satan. We think if we acknowledge Satan something might be required of us. That scares us. It is easier to blame God than to accept responsibility. We have been casting blame since the Garden of Eden. That comes easily to us.

"Poor God, how often He is blamed for all the suffering in the world. It's like praising Satan for allowing all the good that happens."
—E.A. Bucchianeri, *Brushstrokes of a Gadfly*

We must learn to see behind every sickness, every breakup, every conflict, every lie, and every evil thing. There might be a spirit of infirmity behind sickness, or a spirit of poverty behind those who are poor. Sometimes we look through judgmental eyes rather than our spiritual eyes. We should not take Satan out of the picture. He is responsible for some of our troubles. *My people perish because of lack of knowledge," (Hosea 4:6).* We must put on our armor (Ephesians 6:10-18). We must change our thinking.

This is taken from my African journal. I met an extraordinary man. I felt small, somehow, in the presence of this life, in the presence of this person who had changed the world around him.

Issaih was crippled from birth. A child who is defective is often neglected and must fight to survive.

I met Issaih outside of a little schoolhouse near Cheriponi. He rode on a hand pedaled wheel chair. All of the wheel chairs in this part of the country have a bicycle chain and pedals. They are situated in front of the person's chest. He had a big smile on his face. I watched as one by one people showed their respect by taking his right hand or by bowing or bending low and tipping their head to the ground. As I approached him, his little shriveled legs and feet were curled under his seat. I could have put my hand around his thigh and my fingers and thumb would have touched.

Gladys introduced me and translated. I asked Issaih, "What was it like for you, growing up?"

He said, "I was living in Salaga. It was very hard. I was hungry much of the time. I could not get the things that I needed." He patted his stomach.

"You struggled when you were a child?" I inquired.

"Yes, I did not have a wheel chair so I pulled myself with my elbows and dragged myself wherever I needed to go. I was always sick and got sicker as I grew older. I could not eat and grew very thin. I was in constant pain all over and felt like I was dying."

"What did you do?"

"I was a Muslim and I went to the Mosque and prayed to Allah to heal me. Each time I went, I felt empty on the inside." He touched his chest. "I knew this was not the place for me. My sickness grew worse. Those in the mosque became frustrated with me and told me to go and see the fetish priest."

"Did you go?" I asked.

He said, "No, I told them that I would not go. I knew many people who went to the fetish priest and none of them were healed. I did not have money to spend on the medicine and relics, either."

I asked. "What did you do?"

He continued, "I went to a Christian church. The pastor there dealt with a spirit of infirmity and prayed for me to be healed. I was immediately healed of my sickness. There was great pain before, but then there was no more pain. I gave my life to Jesus Christ and I felt new again. It was Jesus Christ who healed me." His face lit up!

Gladys and I rejoiced with him.

He said, "I could not stay there in that place anymore. Some of my family had moved to Cheriponi, so I decided to take Jesus to my family."

"Did they accept you?" I asked.

"No, it was very hard at first. No one wanted to talk to me. I didn't have food to eat. Jesus helped me. He gave me what I needed. Jesus has been so good to me. Now I raise Guinea hens and fowl."

"By fowl, do you mean chickens?"

He answered, "Yes. Now if I need some money I catch a hen or a fowl and go and sell it."

I asked, "Did you lead your family to Jesus?"

He smiled again, "Yes, all of them."

"How many people have you lead to the Lord since you have moved to Chereponi?" I queried.

He thought for a while and then said, "I am not sure, but I have planted twelve churches. Most of them have around one hundred people who attend."

Amazed, I asked, "You planted twelve churches by going around on your wheel chair?"

"Yes, I did. I was much stronger then and I could travel the miles easily. I am older now and do not have the strength that I had then, so I have no way of getting there anymore. People ask me to come preach and pray with them, but I cannot go. I want to go so much, but I cannot. I am praying that Jesus will provide transportation for me so I can continue His work."

I said, "I will pray with you, too."

"I am ready all of the time. I travel with my Bible right here with me." He picked up his new testament Bible to show me. He was so proud of his Bible. The Old Testament has not been translated into his Dagumba language yet.

I invited him to stay and be a part of our women's training event that day. He was very excited that we had asked him. He put a pair of flip-flops on his hands instead of his feet, slid himself out of his seat and on to the ground. Using his arms like crutches, he curled his crippled legs and feet under him and swung himself back and forth as he moved forward.

As the day wore on, I noticed him as he climbed back on to his chair and rode away. He came back later with two young boys riding his chair with him. They had loaded twelve yams and two live Guinea hens. These gifts were presented to us as we were leaving.

Charity told me he said, "This is because they are proud that you taught them the Bible in a way that they could understand. You did a very good job!"

They were kind to all of us. He had given us two of his hens. I was overwhelmed and thanked him.

One woman asked if we could travel to a nearby village to pray for her daughter. She said, "The top of her head is always in pain. We cannot put anything on it. She has been many times to the fetish priests but it has gotten worse. A Christian has never prayed for her."

I asked Issaih if he would like to go with us. It made his day! He put his flip-flops on his hands, moved to the van and then used all of his strength to climb aboard.

When we got to the woman's hut, she sat down on a grass mat and he sat next to her. We all prayed, and spoke healing over her in Jesus' Name. He shared with her about the love that he has for Jesus Christ and about the things that Christ has done for him in his life. I would have given anything to understand all of what they were saying. As we were leaving, the woman said, "The top of my head feels like it is on fire!"

Issaih said, "That is the healing power of God. You are healed in Jesus' Name."

As we dropped him off at his hut, he had such joy when he said, "I cannot express the love I have for Jesus. He has done so much for me!"

As we drove away Gladys said, "Here is a man who is crippled and wants to go and do things for Christ, but can't. There are many people who have two good legs and could do things for Christ, but won't."

It is interesting that the name Issaih in the Dagumba language means "Jesus." Issaih has become a living Jesus for the people there in Cheriponi.

Jesus is the standard. Jesus never made anyone sick. He never hurt anyone. Jesus went about doing good things. He went about healing all who were sick or oppressed.

...God anointed Jesus of Nazareth with the Holy Spirit and power, and how He went about doing good and healing all who were under the power of the devil, because God was with Him.
—Acts 10:38, NIV (emphasis mine)

A very sick young woman (I will call her Martha) called me and asked me to come to the hospital and pray with her. The doctors said the situation was serious, but not hopeless.

We visited for a while and then I asked, "Do you believe it is God's will for you to be healed?"

She said, "Yes, I believe He can heal me."

That was not what I had asked. I enquired again, "You said you believe that He can heal you, but do you believe that it is His <u>will</u> for you to be healed?"

She paused thoughtfully and then said, "Yes, I think so."

I prayed with Martha several times and we read scripture together. Each time I left, there was a marked improvement in her health. She felt loved and encouraged. I was sad sometime later, however, when I heard that she had died. Although she said she believed that it was God's will to heal her, her behavior did not show it. She consistently talked with others about her illness. She dwelled on her impending death. Perhaps the first answer Martha gave me was the one she really believed. She believed the Lord <u>could</u> heal her. I am not sure she believed He <u>would</u>. It makes a big difference!

Religion provides the tools that we need to have a relationship with God and the opportunity to be a part of a family of like-minded believers. If we do not have an engaging relationship with God where He regularly challenges us, it is easy to lose our passion and enthusiasm. When we go through the motions of church and attend primarily for social reasons, we began a slow fade.

It is easy to mosey down the path of routine and eventually settle into a more pasteurized form of religion. We become disillusioned and feel empty. We wonder what happened to the excitement we once had and we struggle to be connected to God once again. It is easy to get lost in legalism at this point, and feel as though we must earn the favor of God. It never fails that about this time Satan will drop a crisis into our laps and we, in desperation, cry out to God. We feel very far from Him, however, and our faith wavers. We struggle with unbelief and become desperate and afraid. We feel vulnerable and helpless. We forget everything we have learned and we give in to our emotions. Our prayers are as weak as milk toast and we wind up begging and pleading. We have lost our faith, so we reach out to hang on to someone else's faith. Hopelessness hinders the healing process (Romans 3:21-26).

I know Martha loved the Lord and was a good person, but I wonder if she slipped into a life of religious complacency and eventually lost her faith. When her crisis came and she needed the strength and fortitude to fight, her tank was empty and she did not have the wherewithal to step into the battle. She did not want to pick up her slingshot and face her Goliath.

It is important that we devise strategies in order to face our battles head on. We must position ourselves to receive healing. There should never be a separation of any kind. We can live a life of expectation if we have a good relationship with <u>God</u> and <u>others</u> and if we truly love <u>ourselves</u>.

One of the teachers of the law came and heard them debating. Noticing that Jesus had given them a good answer, he asked him, "Of all the commandments, which is the most important?

"The most important one," answered Jesus, "is this: 'Hear, O Israel, the Lord our God, the Lord is one. Love the Lord your <u>God</u> with all your heart and with all your soul and with all your mind and with all your strength.' The second, like it, is this: 'Love your <u>neighbor</u> as <u>yourself</u>.' There is no other commandment greater than these."
—Mark 12:30-31 (emphasis mine)

We cannot live as the world lives and blatantly sin. We must live for Christ, place our faith in Him and honor Him. It is important to walk in forgiveness. Knowing that our sins are forgiven, and that we are made right with God, is essential if we are to freely receive healing. We must know, without a shadow of a doubt, that Jesus shed His blood for the <u>forgiveness of sins.</u>

While they were eating, Jesus took bread, and when he had given thanks, he broke it and gave it to his disciples, saying, "Take and eat; this is my body."
Then he took a cup, and when he had given thanks, he gave it to them, saying, "Drink from it, all of you. This is my blood of the covenant, which is poured out for many for the <u>forgiveness of sins</u>.
—Matthew 26:26-28 (emphasis mine)

We can confidently go to God about everything.

The Lord told us that we would have difficult times. Rain falls on the good and the bad equally. We must contend with Satan, our enemy. We wrestle with our flesh and are forced to deal with the consequences. We live in a broken world. People who are hurting surround us. Hurting people hurt people. We react or respond out of our wounds. If we do not know who God is, it is easy to become angry and blame Him. We then turn our backs on God, the very person who can take us out of our misery. God is falsely accused for everything bad that happens in the world. We should be angry with Satan. He is our enemy. We should resist him and stand firm!

> *Be alert and of sober mind. Your enemy the devil prowls around like a roaring lion looking for someone to devour. Resist him, standing firm in the faith, because you know that the family of believers throughout the world is undergoing the same kind of sufferings.*
> *—1 Peter 5:8-9 (emphasis mine)*

Satan works to destroy our lives. He thought he could deceive Jesus by tempting Him in the desert (Matthew 4). That is what Satan does. Jesus did not fall for it. The Bible says we do not wrestle against flesh and blood but against principalities, powers and wickedness

> *Finally, my brethren, be strong in the Lord and in the power of His might. Put on the whole armor of God that you may be able to stand against the wiles of the devil. For we do not wrestle against flesh and blood, but against principalities, against powers, against the rulers of the darkness of this age, against spiritual hosts of wickedness in the heavenly places.*
> *—Ephesians 6:10-12, KJV (emphasis mine)*

Satan is behind many of our difficulties.

God wants to bless our lives but let's be honest; it is not easy to do the will of God. The more we step out in faith, the harder the will of God becomes. Our dreams get bigger. More demands are placed upon us. We pray hard; we work harder. (Yes, a lot of hard work.) Our faith stretches. Our lives may become uncomfortable and inconvenienced. The blessings of God follow, however, and we ride on a tidal wave of joy to the next act of obedience. Just as sin complicates our lives in negative ways, the blessings of God complicate our lives in positive ways.

If we ask God to help us live lives of faith, it is imperative that we know what we are asking and that we agree to it whole heartedly. A "whatever will be, will be" way of thinking is not Biblical. Yes, God is sovereign. He has self-determined freedom and supreme control. He used His authority and set things in motion to work for our benefit. God is in partnership with us; however, and we each have responsibility.

"The will of God is not something you add to your life. It's a course you choose. You either line yourself up with the Son of God...or you capitulate to the principle which governs the rest of the world."

—Elisabeth Elliot

Chapter Fifteen

FISH, PUMPKIN SEEDS, AND A CAR

"If we don't plant the right things, we will reap the wrong things. It goes without saying. And you don't have to be, you know, a brilliant biochemist and you don't have to have an IQ of 150. Just common sense tells you to be kind, ninny, fool. Be kind."

—Maya Angelou

Christians have a duel citizenship on this earth. John admonishes us, "Do not love the world…" (1 John 2:15, NIV). This means we should not love the (worldly) system that is void of God's influence. Jesus Christ must be the center of a Christian's world. We should never let Christ become a casual outside influence.

God's kingdom is more than real estate or a floating heavenly realm. God's kingdom is in the prayers that find their way to God. His kingdom is part of the constant, unseen battle between the His angels and Satan's demons. We notice His kingdom when the little old lady takes homemade brownies and visits the brothel, or when the college student stops to change someone's flat tire, or in that anonymous check we get in the mail when we have bills we cannot pay. We find God's kingdom in a mother's love for her child. It is in a million ordinary, random acts of love and kindness. We find His kingdom in sincere, uninterrupted worship. Yes, God's kingdom is all around us.

The laws of one kingdom, however, do not work in another kingdom. I lived in Ireland for a time. I had an American driver's license that let the authorities know that I knew how to drive. The driving rules in Ireland, however, are different from American driving rules. I needed to learn the Irish way of doing things.

This principle works the same way spiritually. We cannot use the rules of one kingdom (the worldly kingdom) to tap into the resources of another kingdom (God's kingdom). It works the other way around. We gain access to the resources of God's kingdom by following His principles. A life of faith is one of living within the resources of God's kingdom. In God's world it is not human need that pulls on resources, it is faith. It is stewardship. It is obedience. It is using correctly what God has given. Many people wait for God to show up and do something. Faith is so much more than that. God is moved by human need; so moved, in fact, that He sent His Son Jesus who paid a terrible price in order to settle every issue. Everything was taken care of at Calvary.

In Matthew 14 we find this story: A large group of people gathered to hear Jesus. They were hungry. Jesus took five loaves of bread and two fish that a little boy had offered. Five thousand people were fed. There were twelve baskets of left overs when they were finished. The disciples looked at the fish and saw lack. They did not think the meager food the boy offered was enough to feed so many people. Jesus saw it differently. For Him, what the boy offered was enough. Jesus glimpsed into God's kingdom and saw an immediate and unlimited supply. He gave thanks in advance of the miracle. How many of us can look at lack and can see a miracle?

In this world, our leaders look at the resources that are available and distribute those resources based on the most needy. Often times, the squeaky wheel gets the grease. That is not God's way of doing things, however. Jesus tells a parable of a man who gave each of his servant's money to invest. One servant was afraid and buried the money instead. The man was displeased with the servant and took the money that he had buried from him and gave it to the servant who had made the most money from his investments (Matthew 25: 14-29). We often give in to fear and ignore the promptings of the Holy Spirit. We are selfish with our time and resources because we are unsure of the return we might get from our investment.

God put in place a principle called reciprocity: Whatever a man sows is what he shall reap.

> *Do not be deceived: God cannot be mocked. A man reaps what he sows. The one who sows to please their sinful nature, from that nature will reap destruction; the one who sows to please the spirit, from the Spirit will reap eternal life. Let us not become weary in doing good, for at the proper time we will reap a harvest if we do not give up.*
> *—Galatians 6:7-9, NIV (emphasis mine)*

If a man sows corn, he gets corn. A pumpkin seed will not grow a watermelon. It is a principle that cannot be changed. If we sow bad things, we will reap bad things. If we sow good things, we will reap good things. If we sow sin, we reap sin. It is a principle; it does not forget. He who sows to the flesh will reap corruption. He who sows to the spirit will reap life everlasting. Let us not be weary in well doing, for in due season we will reap a harvest. Patience is required. There is the planting of the seed, the growing of the seed, a little more time, usually a little more time and then eventually a harvest. The Lord says the Word will not return empty.

> *"For my thoughts are not your thoughts, neither are your ways my ways," declares the Lord. "As the heavens are higher than the earth, so are my ways higher than your ways and my thoughts than your thoughts. As the rain and the snow come down from heaven, and do not return to it without watering the earth and making it bud and flourish, so that it yields seed for the sower and bread for the eater, so is my word that goes out from my mouth: It will not return to me empty, but will accomplish what I desire and achieve the purpose for which I sent it.*
> *—Isaiah 55:8-11 (emphasis mine)*

Sow the Word of God and you will have a harvest. Sometimes harvest comes a little quicker that we anticipate.

My sister Stormy came to me one day and said, "I really need a new car and I have asked the Lord to provide one for me. I have very little money. I need a miracle. Would you come into agreement with me and pray as well?"

I assured her, "I will be happy to come into agreement and pray with you."

Later that week I noticed a for sale sign on a car in the front yard of a young couple in my Bible study class. At church that week I said to the couple, "I noticed you have a car for sale. Does it run well? Why are you selling it?"

She said, "It runs very well. I drove it all through college. We have decided to sell it in order to pay off part of our student loans."

I said, "My sister is looking for a new car. Would you mind talking to her about it?" She said, "My husband and I will be happy to."

Stormy drove the car and loved it. They gave her the asking price and, to be honest, she really could not afford it. Nevertheless she said, "Thank you so much. Let me pray about it and let you know something in the morning."

Stormy talked with me and said, "I love the car, but I cannot afford it. Please keep praying."

Well, that night, the Lord began to work on the hearts of the young couple. The Lord spoke to them individually. The next morning they shared with each other what the Lord had told them. They were in complete agreement. They called Stormy, "We prayed about it and have decided to give you our car."

Stormy said, "Give it to me? I thought you wanted to pay off some of your student loans with the money you would get from the car."

They said, "Yes, we were going to, but the Lord told us to sow the car. He told us to give it to you. We are going to do what the Lord told us to do and trust that He will provide the money to pay off the loans." Stormy was elated! Praise Jesus!

On the following Sunday morning during the worship service I did a short children's sermon on Philippians 4:19 (NIV): "And my God will meet your needs according to His glorious riches in Christ Jesus." I told the story of how God had answered my sister's need by giving her a new car. I did not mention the name of the couple who had given her the car, however. As I finished a closing prayer I looked up in the balcony of the church and noticed that the father of the young woman who had donated the car had tears running down his face. It struck me as odd because that was not characteristic of him.

I enquired the next time that I saw her. "I noticed that your dad was crying during the children's message on Sunday. Is everything all right?"

She laughed and said, "Yes, you will never guess what happened! We went to my parents' house after church that day and my dad said, 'I heard what Misty said during the children's message. That car she was talking about was your car, wasn't it?'"

"I said, 'Yes, Dad, it was.'

"He said, 'I thought you were going to use the money to pay off some of your student loans.'

"I told him, 'We were going to, but we prayed about it and the Lord told us to give the car away instead. I know it doesn't make sense, Dad, but it is something we felt strongly that we had to do.'"

She said, "I wasn't sure how he was going to take it."

He asked, "How much do you owe on your student loans?"

"I told him and he did the most unexpected thing. He was so moved that he got his checkbook and wrote a check for me that paid off all student loans! Selling the car would have covered only a small part of our debt. Now, we have paid off the entire debt. We sowed only a little seed, but we got a great harvest! Can you believe it? We are so thankful! Praise God!"

Stormy loved the car! It was in such good condition that she drove it for years. Sowing to the good reaps the good.

It is wise to keep the harvest in mind. As Christians, we are living for something that is ahead of us. This should be encouraging. The harvest never comes before the planting. Spiritually, it is the same. It is a terrific investment program, but sometimes it feels endless. The hardest part is dealing with life day-to-day. There will always be one more load of clothes to wash. One more diaper to change. One more bill to pay. One more meal to prepare. One more parent-teacher meeting. We are all laying down our lives for another generation. The fruit of our labor may not even be seen until our children are much older. We are living for another place, another person, and another generation. We will not get gypped. We will just have to wait for the harvest.

"You should first follow the plow if you want to dance the harvest jig."

—Ken Follett, *World Without End*

Jesus understands this. He lived in obscurity as a carpenter for most of His life. He did not begin His ministry until He was thirty, when John the Baptist baptized him in the river Jordan. There a voice came from heaven saying, *"This is my beloved son in whom I am well pleased,"* (Matthew 3:17). His Father was pleased with Him before He had performed any miracles, healed anyone or gathered the disciples.

I talked with a well-dressed lady who ran a successful business. "Misty," she asked, "Why does God bless me even though you and I both know that I am sinning? I am sleeping around [there were many men in her life], but my business is doing well and I think that I am just fine." She was totally deceived. She believed that even though she was fornicating, it was all right with God because her business was doing well.

If we are blatantly sinning and God is blessing us, it is because He hopes that His blessings and mercy will lead us to repentance. He wants us to bring our hearts back to Him before He brings down the rod. We will reap what we sow. I grew up in a farming area, so let me put it this way. If you are living in deliberate sin, do not look now, but that sound you hear behind you is the combine gaining ground.

Sooner or later, each of us reaps what we have sown. The Bible tells the story of Jacob, who deceived his father by pretending to be his older brother (Genesis 25–28). He wanted his father to bless him instead of his older brother Esau who had the birthright, which belongs to the older male child. It worked, too. When his deception was discovered, he ran away. He fell in love with a beautiful girl named Rachel and worked for seven years before her father Laban would allow him to marry her. On the wedding day, Jacob lifted the veil and discovered that he been deceived; he had married the older daughter Leah instead.

He had sowed deception and he reaped deception. He pretended to be the older, when he was the younger. He wanted to marry the younger, but got the older.

After having Naboth killed, King Ahab and Queen Jezebel took Naboth's vineyard. They thought they would get away with it. The prophet Elijah, however, told them they would reap what they had sowed. He told Ahab that he would die in the same place that Naboth had been killed. Ahab's blood would be spilled and the dogs would lick it up. Ahab did not believe that it would come true, but decided to stay away from that place, anyway. When Ahab was fatally wounded, he told his chariot driver to take him out of the battle. The driver took him right to that spot where Naboth had died. Ahab died there in the chariot. When they washed the chariot, the dogs licked up the blood (1 Kings 21). Payday is coming someday. God is not mocked. We will reap what we sow.

Let me encourage you. When you plant an apple seed, a whole tree of apples will grow. When you plant a kernel of wheat, a whole stalk will appear. It works that way spiritually, too. The good things we sow will reap more blessings than we can imagine! The Lord is looking for ways to bless us! He is fair. He loves us more than we can know!

If we spend our lives loving, love will come back to us. If we spend our lives giving, we will reap a generous harvest. God meets our needs by using other people. If we need money, God might speak to someone's heart and He will bless us with money.

I met a homeless family one time and arranged temporary housing for them through the ministry where I volunteered. Both parents were unemployed. They had no money and were very hungry. My heart broke for the three small children, who looked pitiful. I talked with the father, "Someone is bringing food that should last a couple of days. We will also provide a little money for other things.

He shook his head disapprovingly, "No, we do not take handouts."

He must have been terribly embarrassed about the awful situation he and his family were facing, but I was shocked at his stubbornness. Would he be prideful enough to deny his hungry wife and children? I asked, "Have you ever seen money growing on trees?"

He said, "No."

I explained, "I haven't either. God loves you and wants to help you and your family, but His provision is not going to grow on a tree or fall from the sky. Provision is going to come through people. Saying no to the person God is using to help you is saying no to God. You may want to reconsider your thinking."

Although reluctantly, he let us help him and his family. He later found a job. God uses others to bless us and we must set our pride aside and position our hearts to receive. It is hard to reap when we are always turning away from what God is trying to give us.

"Any fear associated with giving to God's kingdom is irrational. It's on par with a farmer who, out of fear of losing his seed, refuses to plant his."
—Andy Stanley, *Fields Of Gold*

Chapter Sixteen

The Goodyear Blimp, Greeting Cards, and a Horse and Buggy

"Timing is so important! If you are going to be successful in dance, you must be able to respond to rhythm and timing. It's the same in the Spirit. People who don't understand God's timing can become spiritually spastic, trying to make the right things happen at the wrong time. They don't get His rhythm – and everyone can tell they are out of step. They birth things prematurely, threatening the very lives of their God-given dreams."

—T. D. Jakes

As I mentioned, I lived in the Northern part of Ghana, West Africa for a time, working with a ministry and helping plant churches among the unreached people groups. I made several friends while I was there that I talk with quite often.

The northern villages are impoverished. The people wear the only clothes they own. They eke out an existence by hoeing fields using short handle hoes and planting small crops. These families live in little mud huts with thatched roofs that they have made themselves. They sleep on mats made of straw they have woven together. Some women walk seven or eight miles in one direction each day in order to haul water for drinking, cooking and bathing.

It is interesting that although they may not have running water and electricity, almost everyone has a cell phone. They use prepaid minutes and turn on their phones only if it is absolutely necessary. The people who live in the surrounding villages make the long journey into town on market day to sell cassava, rice, millet and other things they have made or grown. They stop by the mission to charge their cell phones. The mission church has electricity, although it is not very dependable.

Now that I am back in America, I receive phone calls from my friends in Ghana quite often. We talk about how things are in Ghana and we pray for each other. It is such a blessing! My friend Felix called one day and asked, "Misty, would you mind asking the Lord to provide the equivalent in Ghana cedi's to fifty American dollars?"

Felix is not the kind of person who asks for money, so I knew this was important to him. My friends in Ghana had all mentioned how difficult things there were for them. Even rice was too expensive for them to buy. Everyone was really struggling. So I did not ask him for any details.

When I talked with him later that week, he still had not received the money. I asked, "How soon do you need to have the money?"

He answered, "We must have it by Monday."

I inquired, "We?"

He said, "Yes, the money is not for me. It is for someone who needs to pay his school fees. If he does not pay on Monday, they will not allow him to go to school. The church promised to help pay the fees, but they do not have the money. I promised I would help, but I do not have the money either."

I understood what they were going through. I have been living by faith for several years and the Lord is faithful to meet all of my needs. Those needs are always met in a timely fashion, but rarely ever early.

I said, "Felix, I would like to help, but I do not have money right now. Let's pray and ask the Lord to give fifty dollars to me and I will, in turn, wire it to you." We prayed together over the phone.

As the Lord would have it, I got a call from the church where I attend. The lady in the office said, "Someone left an envelope here for you back in December and we keep forgetting to give it to you. Would you mind picking it up the next time that you are here?"

The envelope contained a Christmas card and a crisp fifty dollar bill. It was February now. This was more than happenstance and I knew it!

I called Felix, "Guess what? I have the money and I am wiring it to you right now. Even with the time difference between the States and Ghana, your friend should still be able to make his school payment deadline."

Felix assured me the young man would make it there in time. Then he told me the rest of the story. He said, "I did not tell you this, but my friend was a Muslim who gave his life to Jesus and became a Christian. His family has rejected him and he has lost everything. I will call him now and let him know that we have the money that he needs."

I wired the money to Felix and called to give him the reference number of the transfer. Felix said, "I just talked with my friend. At the moment you were wiring the money, he was with his pastor and others in their little church praying for the Lord to provide the money to pay his school fees. I was able to tell him that God is faithful and that He has provided!"

I told my friend Sheila, who had given me the money, "You are never going to believe how the Lord used your money!" She cried. I had been to the church dozens of times. If I had known about the money I would have used it for something else. God had bigger, better plans! How humbling it is to be used by God. How humbling it was to be a part of God's plan and to make a difference in the life of a new Christian who, because of his faith, had lost everything.

This experience humbled me and reminded me of how important timing is to God. We must remind ourselves that God does not see things the way we see things. He sees the whole picture. Suppose we are sitting on bleachers along a parade route. If we look in front of us, what do we know for sure? We have seen all of the floats, bands, and clowns that have already passed by. We see what is happening in front of us at that moment. We may even have an idea of what is coming. We know Santa is at the end of the parade, after all, but we cannot see everything all of the time.

God is not limited in that way. God would be in the Goodyear blimp, floating above the parade. He sees what has already passed, what is present, and what is to come. He can interact with anything or anyone at anytime, if He wanted to.

This became very evident to me as I watched and was a part of the things that God was doing in my friend Helen's life.

When Helen was in her eighties and living in the small apartment where I met her, her answering machine was always full of prayer requests and invitations to visit churches. Her days were filled with visits with people who wanted to learn from her. People came to her for prayer and to be in her presence. Over time, her little body was worn out. The Lord told her to move to a Fair Haven Retirement Community in the Northern part of Birmingham. He said, "Helen, get rid of the phone, give away your television and do not read newspapers or magazines. I want you all to myself. Do not be concerned with seeing people. I will send those to you who need you. You be at peace and rest." She took Him at His Word and did what He asked.

Helen did not have enough money to live there, but she trusted the Lord would provide. I was visiting her one day and she said, "I want to go downstairs to the beauty parlor and get my hair done. Will you go with me?"

Agreeing, I said, "I will be happy to."

"Let's stop by the bookkeeper and make sure I have enough money to pay for my hairdo." We took the elevator and then walked to the accountant's office. "I want to get my hair fixed. Do I have enough money?"

I thought the woman was going to fall off of her chair laughing, "Helen, you have more money than you can spend in two lifetimes. Go and get your hair done!"

When Helen moved into the retirement center a doctor stopped by and said, "I'd like to start a Fountain of Life Fund for Helen Wright and contribute $500 a month." Another man dropped by later and made a commitment, then another and another. All of them kept their promises to provide and Helen never thought about money again. She was obedient and took no thought except about doing what Jesus wanted her to do. She was faithful to Him and He was faithful to her.

One day I was driving to Birmingham on a shopping trip. I was going to visit Helen when all of my chores were finished, even though she did not know I was coming. The last stop on my "to do" list was the Baptist Bible Bookstore. God, however, had other plans for me.

As I approached Birmingham the Lord spoke to me. He said, "Get off at this exit and go to the Christian bookstore."

I had my "to do" list in mind and said, "Lord, I was going to go to a couple of other places before I went to the bookstore."

He quickened my spirit and said, "Misty, get off at this exit and go to the Baptist Bible Bookstore."

I replied with a smile, "Yes, sir!"

I parked the car, went inside and stood there for a moment. "Okay, I am here Lord. What would you like for me to do?"

He said, "Go over to the card section and purchase some greeting cards. I will show you which ones to get."

I walked over to card aisle. The store was having a sale on greeting cards. I thought, "God probably had these folks put them on sale just for me."

He said, "Get the boxed card sets." They were on sale, two for one. I picked out several: birthday, anniversary, congratulations, and thinking of you condolence sets. I did just as the Lord directed.

Then I asked, "Now what do I do?"

He said, "Go ahead and pay for them." I did as He asked. The lady put all of the cards in an easy to carry large white bag with a handle.

I asked, "Okay, Lord, now what would you like for me to do?"

He said, "Go on to visit Helen."

I carried the bag to her little second floor room and knocked on the door. You would not believe what happened next.

Helen answered the door, took one look at me and then began to do a little dance around her room, "Praise the Lord! He has answered our prayer! Praise the Lord, He has answered our prayer."

I looked into the room and saw Polly sitting there. I had met Polly on an earlier visit. She was older than Helen, but sharp as a tack. Polly looked puzzled. She was not the only puzzled one. I was left standing in the hall while Helen danced her little jig. When Helen finally came to me, she took the bag without looking into it. Still smiling, she placed the bag on Polly's lap. Only then did she invite me inside.

By the time I entered the room, Polly was holding the boxes of greeting cards in her hands as though they were gold. She was dumbfounded. She said over and over, "I don't believe it. I just don't believe it. I don't believe it!"

After a few pleasantries, Polly excused herself, took the cards and left. I said, "Ms. Helen, what in the world is happening?"

Helen said, "When I moved here, I asked the Lord for a new best friend and then I met Polly, but she was not a Christian. I was so excited because I love talking with new people about Jesus. The Lord told me not to tell Polly about Him because He knew she would not listen. Her heart is hardened. He is going to allow her to see three miracles so that she will believe."

Helen continued, "I said, 'Okay, Lord, you just tell me what to do and I will do it.'"

Polly is the hospitality chairman on the retirement community council. One of her jobs is sending greeting cards to residents each month. Polly told Helen, "I am going to get on the bus, and go on down to Bruno's and buy greeting cards."

Helen said, "The Lord whispered in my spirit, 'Tell Polly not to do that. Tell her I am going to provide the greeting cards.'"

"So I said, 'Polly you don't have to go to the store because the Lord is going to provide the cards.' Polly was hesitant, but agreed.

"As the time for the council meeting drew closer, however, Polly was nervous and impatient. 'Helen, I can just go to the store.'

"Encouraging her to be patient I said, 'Polly, wait a little longer, because God is going to provide the cards that you need.'"

Helen was excited as she told me, "And Misty, this morning you showed up just in time. The meeting is Saturday and Polly was going to get on that bus! And God sent you."

I said, "So that is why she looked so astonished and kept saying, 'I don't believe it, I just don't believe it, I don't believe it.'"

Helen said, "Yes. That was miracle number one."

A short time later I visited Helen again. I inquired about Polly. Helen said, "You know Polly has lots of money. Her room has nice furniture. I visited her one day and saw a beautiful, nicely framed picture hanging on the wall. I had been having trouble with my eyesight, so I took the little picture into my hands to look at it more closely. As I held it, the hanger on the back broke. When I realized what had happened, I was sick about it. I took the picture over to Polly to show her.

"I said, 'Polly, I am so sorry. I wanted to have a closer look, but when I did the hanger on the back broke.'

"I turned the picture over to show it to Polly and the Lord spoke to me at that moment, 'Helen, go downstairs now and take the picture with you. You will see a man who is just leaving and he will help you.'

"I said to Polly, 'The Lord says that I am to go downstairs because someone is there who...'

"The Lord interrupted before I had finished explaining and said, 'Helen, go right now, this moment!'"

Helen said hurriedly, "Polly I have to go right now, but I will be back."

When Helen arrived downstairs and rounded the corner at the front of the building, she saw a man leaving through the automatic double doors.

Helen said, "Excuse me, sir. Excuse me, sir. I have a problem, can you help me?"

The man said, "I don't know, but I will help if I can."

Helen took the little picture over to him, showed him the broken piece and explained what had happened. The man said, "Oh goodness, this type of hanger is difficult to find. It must be special ordered. But hang on a minute, I think I have one in my truck." Helen happened to be speaking to the owner of a framing shop!

She was overjoyed! The man repaired the picture. Helen took it up stairs and gave it to Polly. Polly held it in her hands and said, "I don't believe it, I just don't believe it, I don't believe it!"

Helen said, "Yes, that was miracle number two."

Amazed at the stories of God's faithfulness, I left feeling encouraged. I knew there would be a third miracle and looked forward to hearing about it on my next visit. Before I left, however, I inquired about Helen's eye. I noticed blood pooling toward the bottom. I asked, "Ms. Helen, what is wrong with your eye?"

She said, "I have been having trouble with my eye, so I went to the doctor. It was an awful experience."

I asked, "What happened?"

She said, "Misty, the doctor's office was one of the coldest places I have ever visited. The air conditioner thermostat was turned down so low that the room was icy. The people who worked in the office were not friendly. I felt like a cow being herded through."

I said, "I am so sorry."

She continued, "Well, I went into the little room where the procedure was going to be done. The doctor came in and said, 'Ms. Wright, I want you to come over to this machine and put your chin on this pedestal. I am going to stick a needle into your eye and repair the problem.' I did as she asked. It was a terrible experience! It put my body into shock! My friend drove me home and I was in bed for three days."

My stomach flip-flopped just thinking about it. "Goodness, Ms. Helen. I hope you don't mind my asking, but I see blood inside your eye now. It isn't supposed to be there, is it?"

Helen said, "No. As a matter of fact, I have to go back to the doctor. She is going to do the procedure all over again."

Helen and I had a good visit and then I left. I came back later in the month and asked about her appointment with the eye doctor.

Helen said, "Well, I knew I had to go back to the doctor and have that terrible procedure done again and to be honest I was afraid. I did not want to go through that again. It was all I could think about. I was whining and complaining to God about it. There was not much faith there, to be honest with you; but the Lord knew my heart.

"He spoke to me and asked, 'Helen, who should you be praying for and have your mind on beside yourself?'

"I stopped and thought a moment and said, 'Lord I need to be praying for that lady doctor. The one who did my procedure.'

"The Lord said, 'That's right.'

"I began to pray for her and the more I prayed the more the Lord put a love in my heart for her. Before long I couldn't wait to see her."

She said, "Misty, isn't it amazing when the Lord does that?"

I said, "It sure is. What happened next?"

Helen continued, "The time came for the appointment and a friend drove me to the doctor's office. I went inside and the place still felt so cold.

"The doctor came into the room and said, 'Ms. Wright, come over to the machine and put your chin on this pedestal...'

"Then the Lord interrupted, 'Helen, I want you to go over to her, wrap your arms around her, kiss her on the face, tell her that I love her and you love her and that you have been praying for her.'

"I said, 'Lord, do I have to kiss her on the face?' But I did what the Lord asked. I wrapped by arms around her, gave her a big hug, kissed her on the cheek then said, 'I want you to know that I have been praying for you. I love you and the Lord loves you, too.' She began to cry and cry. She was so moved. It took a long time for her to regain her composure.

"The doctor said, 'You do not know how much I needed to hear that. I moved to Birmingham to take care of my parents and to start my medical practice. I have poured all of my time and energy into taking care of them and growing my business. My parents have since passed away. I have no friends. I have been so lonely.'"

Helen said, "I talked with her for a little while and she prayed with me and accepted Jesus as her Savior."

I said, "Helen, that is wonderful!"

She said, "That is not all. The doctor asked me once again to put my chin on the pedestal. When she looked in my eye, the Lord had healed it completely! Can you beat that?"

I said, "No, I can't."

She continued, "I received a letter from the doctor a short time later. It said, 'I wanted to thank you. What you did for me changed my life.' The postscript told me that my bill had been paid in full. Isn't that wonderful?"

I said, "Helen that is amazing! Has Polly seen your eye?"

Helen said, "I could hardly wait to tell her about my miracle! She was dumbfounded! She shook her head and said, 'I don't believe it, I just don't believe it, I don't believe it.'"

I asked, "Helen was that miracle number three?"

Helen said, "It sure was!"

I asked, "Helen, why didn't the Lord want you to share your faith with Polly?"

Helen told me Polly's story. When her mother was pregnant with Polly, she did not want a baby. She wanted to have an abortion, but her husband insisted she keep the child. Her unhappy mother was hard to live with. She was not kind to Polly, even nicknaming her "Tempest," a name Polly hated. Her dad was a country doctor who took his black medical bag and, in his horse and buggy, road the countryside taking care of sick people and delivering babies. He loved Polly and she often went with him as he made his rounds. He read the Bible out loud to her as they went. Polly was very familiar with the Bible.

When she was older and married she had two children, but tragedy struck. Her father died, her husband left her, and both of her children were mysteriously found dead. Polly, as you can only imagine, was overwhelmed with grief. She walled up her heart and poured herself into her work. That is why she has so much money. The Lord told Helen He was going to let her see three miracles to change her way of thinking and to open her heart to love again.

Helen later told me that she led Polly to the Lord. They were the best of friends until Polly's death a few years later. Helen was patient and the miracles unraveled in God's timing; Polly learned to love the Lord.

"I wish it need not have happened in my time," said Frodo.

"So do I," said Gandalf, "and so do all who live to see such times. But that is not for them to decide. All we have to decide is what to do with the time that is given us."
—J.R.R. Tolkien, *The Fellowship of the Ring*

Many people are afraid of what will happen to them when they get older.

Time is our friend, although it does not always feel that way. We often feel pressed for time. I wonder how many of us get to the other side of something and say, "I wish I had taken the time."

> I wish I had spent time with my wife;
>> I would not be in the middle of a divorce.
> I wish I had spent time with my children;
>> I would not be estranged from them as adults.
> I wish I had taken time before making that decision;
>> I would not be in litigation right now.
> I wish I had taken the time to work on that friendship;
>> I would still have them as a friend today.
> I wish I had taken the time to develop my relationship with the Lord;

> I would have peace in my life.
> I wish I had taken the time to overcome that fear;
> I would be traveling the world by now.
> I wish I had taken the time to ask the Lord to help me;
> I would not have had to struggle as I have in my life.

If we let time push us around, we will make poor decisions. If we are impatient we will not wait for God to move; we will take things into our own hands instead. God does not always do things in the way we think they should be done, or as quickly as we would like; but His timing is always perfect. Being patient and waiting until God moves, or until He directs us, is the most important thing we can do.

Waiting does not mean sitting down on the couch. We should do the things that we know we need to do until He tells us what to do. God often reveals His will for us through some of the most ordinary things. Once He has directed us, we must put the questions aside and obey immediately. If not, we run the risk of missing the blessings that God has for us. Faith means walking with God one step at a time, one decision at a time, one moment at a time. He seldom reveals things ahead of time. He sometimes reveals enough to give us hope. We then begin to look forward to what is to come. That in itself is empowering.

"As if you could kill time without injuring eternity."
—Henry David Thoreau, "Economy," *Walden*, 1854

Chapter Seventeen

MUD, A FLOCK OF SHEEP AND LABRADOR NAMED MOLLY

Our perceptions are our reality. What we perceive is what we believe, even if it is not true. We should have the correct perception of God. It is important that we know and understand Him. What we think of Him is who He becomes to us. If we think He is a short order cook in the sky, we will simply give him our order, demand a response, and criticize Him if things are not done to our satisfaction. If we think He is a cop trying to catch us doing wrong, we will hide from Him. If we think he is our daddy, reaching out with unconditional love, we will freely go to Him.

If we do not understand who God is and how He communicates, we will not recognize His divine interaction in our lives. We confuse Satan's behavior with God's behavior. This constipates everything. God and Satan are polar opposites. Simply put, God is love and Satan is evil. If we feel guilty, for example, God is not influencing us because God is not a manipulator. Satan, on the other hand, will ladle a heaping portion of guilt on our plate and then add extra helpings of shame and condemnation. Satan burdens us with guilt like a nagging, unbearable toothache in our soul. Satan wants to fill our life with so much helplessness and negativity that we feel sorry for ourselves and roll around in it. He wants us to lie awake in bed at night and replay everything we did wrong during the day. When will we learn that rolling around like a pig in the muck and mud is not a good way to get clean?

"We gather our arms full of guilt as though it were precious stuff. It must be that we want it that way."
—John Steinbeck

I once lived in a two story, stone-hewn house on Sheep Head Peninsula in Southern Ireland. The large picture window just off the kitchen overlooked Bantry Bay. A hillside was nestled between a stone wall at the end of the yard and the eye line of the bay. The hillside was filled with sheep. Those sheep mesmerized me. I learned a lot about Jesus by watching the shepherd interact with his sheep.

The shepherd, carrying his staff, would talk quietly to the sheep as he walked toward them. He would get their attention and then gently lead them to where he wanted them to go. He never tried to force them. If the sheep felt intimidated, they would scatter. <u>God</u> is like that shepherd. He always <u>leads, guides and prompts</u>. He is a gentleman and never forces us to do anything against our will. The Holy Spirit gives a gentle prompt on the inside that guides us. We will know what we need to do. We want to obey because we have a calm assurance deep within and we know that we can trust Him.

A young woman came to me for prayer. She had been deeply betrayed and damaged by her father. When she was a child her father told her he was going to make her strong and teach her the ways of the world. He pressured and sexually abused her and twisted love until she was in so much pain she thought she was going to die. He demanded and manipulated until she began to believe his words were true. She told herself, *Maybe I deserved to be treated this way.*

She cried out for help as a child, but soon learned that no one would listen. Everyone called her crazy. She isolated herself and withdrew into overwhelming loneliness. She learned to survive and to turn the pain off. She thought, *It is better not to feel at all.* Her senses deadened and she forgot her dreams and all of the things that she wanted to do. She pushed the pain deep inside and mindlessly walked through her days. Panic attacks became commonplace and her memory short. As an adult, she looks at her life. Nothing happens day to day now that she should feel bad about, but she still feels numb inside. She begins to believe she is losing her mind.

This poor young woman had fallen prey to Satan's devices. Her father was the tool, a weapon in the hands of Satan. That is what <u>Satan</u> does; he <u>demands, manipulates, controls and pressures</u>. Satan works though other people, circumstances, and situations so he can exact pressure. He uses people to conjure envy, jealousy, strife, and conflict. He causes accidents, disagreements and difficulties. Here are a few of his tactics:

Satan will…
Give us what we crave and then threaten to take it away.
Find ways for people to have leverage over others.
Create situations that will play on our fears.
Instill paranoia that someone is going to leave.
Promote ego so others are controlled for fun.
Use self-pity to draw attention.
Use the fear of being hurt to control situations.
Use poor health to demand things of others.
Force someone to have sex and justify it by saying it was consensual.
Bring confusion so people will not trust their own judgment.
Set a hidden agenda in order to take advantage of people.
Fill our minds with false opinions of what other people think of us.
Say anything to manipulate a conversation.
Encourage false piety like the Pharisees of old.
Deal in half-truths.
Create dependency.

Press children to conform to our expectations.
Create an environment of chaos where manipulation is easy.
Use emotion to pull on heartstrings.

If we have experienced any of these things, Satan's manipulation and control is behind it. If we have been a manipulator, it is Satan who has been whispering in our ears. God will not do any of these things.

I prayed with the young woman who had been damaged by her father. She realized that her impression of God was a reflection of her earthly father's behavior toward her. She forgave her father and began to understand unconditional love. Her life was changed forever.

<u>God is humble, gentle, meek and lowly</u>. These qualities do not mean that He is a doormat. God does not expect us to let people walk all over us and He will not bully to get what He wants.

My friend Kathleen had a beautiful, black Labrador retriever named Molly. Although I was nice to Molly, she did not like me very much. She would stare at me and bark and growl. Molly would hold her favorite old bone in her mouth for the longest time. I was going to play with her, but she was stubborn and would not let me have that old bone. I knew fighting and ripping it from her mouth would never work. We picked up a very large, fresh cow bone at the local farmer's market. I swapped the old, chewed up bone for the meaty, new bone. Molly frantically wagged her tail as she gnawed it. It was only then that she accepted me. We must approach people in the same way, with kindness and humility. That is how God approaches us.

A humble person:
... is always willing to be little.
... is willing to be vulnerable. This shows great strength.
... will speak more of the success of others than of their own success.
... will not look down on other people.
... realizes human wisdom is insufficient.
... knows that someone else's business is none of their business.
... does not try to manage the affairs of others.
... cheerfully accepts criticisms.
... overlooks being slighted or forgotten.
... is calm and does not react when provoked.

... does not make excuses.

Satan, on the other hand, has no meekness or humility. He is hard, harsh, sharp, pressing and very legalistic. Satan knows the Bible in its entirety. He understands what He can legally get away with. He will be terribly harsh and press us until we give in and submit to his will. He is unrelenting!

For example, the Bible tells us that if we wish to be forgiven, we must forgive (Luke 6:37-38). If we refuse to forgive someone, we give Satan a legal foothold into our lives. He will fill us with anger, bitterness, and resentment. When we see that person again, it feels as though he has put salt into our wound. We may act courteous, but on the inside our arms are folded and our blood pressure has sky rocketed!

Satan treats the Bible like it is a law book and forces us to pay attention to our works. We try to save ourselves by keeping the rules. He wants us to focus on the letter of the law and this leaves us looking for loopholes. We try to establish our own righteousness and get lost in a world of trying to be perfect. We fail miserably, of course, so we come up with a game plan. We create a world in which we think we can live. We find ways to bend the rules. Legalism does not make people work harder. It makes them give up. Satan smiles.

"True humility is not thinking less of yourself; it is thinking of yourself less."

—C.S. Lewis, Mere Christianity

God speaks truth and brings clarity. He is the truth. God wants us to have a clear understanding about everything in our lives. The Bible was given for this very purpose. God will go out of His way to ensure we understand.

I ran into an acquaintance at church one time and the Lord spoke to me. He said, "Tell her that the decision she made this morning was the wise decision. Satan is trying to change her mind."

I mustered my courage and said, "You may think this is odd, but the Lord told me to tell you that the decision you made this morning was the wise decision." She sucked in her breath a little and looked very surprised! I continued, "Satan is trying to talk you into changing your mind. Didn't you have peace after you made the decision?"

She said, "Yes, but after a little while I had all of these thoughts running through my head and I began to second guess myself."

I did not ask what it was all about. I simply said, "Well, rest assured you are doing the right thing." She thanked me profusely and then went on her way.

"A lie can travel half way around the world while the truth is putting on its shoes."
—Mark Twain

Satan will go out of his way to make sure we are confused. He deceives, lies and confuses. Satan is a liar and the father of lies (John 8:44). If there is confusion in our lives, Satan is behind it. Satan, with slight of hand, manipulates us so we will live in deception. For example:

We pretend to be someone we are not so that we will be accepted. We become prideful and think of ourselves more highly than we should.
We join cliques in order to be accepted, even if it is not who we are.
We wear a façade in order to cover our vulnerability.
We have delusions about who we are and what we do.
We drag someone along in a relationship when we are only using the person.
We let others influence how we see ourselves.
We believe that other people are responsible for our feelings.
We manipulate the truth to get what we want.

"Pay no attention to the man behind the curtain!"
—L. Frank Baum, *The Wonderful Wizard of Oz*

God is committed and faithful. He patiently endures and is longsuffering. God's Word is His bond! God never gives up on us. He will patiently wait as we learn to walk in obedience and accomplish those things that He has planned for us. We are to follow His example.

Satan, however, is very impatient. He is unfaithful. He pressures us to be fickle about our commitments and unfaithful in our promises. Satan urges us to give up when our expectations do not see immediate results. Satan will poke and cattle prod us until we are jittery and impatient. He wants us to walk away from our commitments. He rejoices when we feel disillusioned and defeated.

God is just. He shows no partiality or favoritism. Thankfully, He treats everyone fairly. It does not matter whether we are good or bad, rich or poor, educated or uneducated, from the city or from the country. He has the same standard for everyone.

Satan is unjust and unfair to everyone. He encourages us to judge others and to think more highly of ourselves than we should. He wants us to belittle and criticize others. We make him happy when we gossip, play favorites and form cliques.

God is excellent! He never compromises. He always goes to the extreme.

"Compromise means to go just a little bit below what you know is right. It's just a little bit, but it's the little foxes that spoil the vine."

—Joyce Meyer

Satan always compromises and urges us to do the same. He enjoys our mediocrity. He wants us to be sloppy. Satan encourages us to be lazy and to procrastinate. Satan loves fence sitters and wishy-washy people.

God is very generous! As a matter of fact, He loves to give. He rejoices when His children prosper. He is not limited, so he can afford to be generous.

Satan pushes us to be stingy, resentful, envious, selfish and jealous. He wants us to be discontent, because discontented people are ungrateful. Satan is the master of discontentment.

God delights in seeing a believer enjoying himself. Parents love laughing, happy children. Our Father feels the same way about us. Joy comes from God.

Satan steals joy and replaces it with self-centered fun, which is disappointing, temporary and fleeting.

God convicts, but never condemns. The Holy Spirit will convict us when we do wrong, but He will never belittle us in the process.

Satan will condemn us. He casts blame to makes us feel guilty. He gives us a false sense of responsibility.

God is Holy, righteous and pure.

Satan is unholy, wicked, evil, impure, and unrighteous.

God is love, which manifests itself in patience, meekness, kindness, humility, unselfishness, goodness, forgiveness, mercy and self-control (Galatians 5:22-23).

Satan holds grudges. He is hateful, bitter, and touchy. He is resentful and easily offended.

God's character, nature and personality are totally different from Satan's. Recognizing the difference between the two is the key to living a life of freedom and victory. It is important to learn to recognize when we are coming into agreement with God or with Satan. Even entertaining the ideas Satan puts into our heads can be a problem. Let me illustrate:

When I was youth director, a lady from a Sunday school class that I attended came to me and asked for help. She said, "I smoke cigarettes and am embarrassed about it. I always smoke outside of my house, because I know second hand smoke is terrible for my family. I am always late for church. I have to have one more cigarette before leaving. I want to stop smoking. Can you help me? Can you pray with me?"

I said, "I would be happy to pray with you and help you deal with the addiction." I called some intercessor friends and we all met. As she prayed and took authority, she was completely delivered of her addiction, in Jesus' Name.

She said, "This is amazing! I do not crave cigarettes anymore. That nicotine taste in my mouth has completely disappeared!" She was beside herself with excitement!

The Lord can deliver us from our addictions, but we still have to break the habit that came with it. People who smoke are used to having something in their hands and on their lips; they feel the loss when it is gone. That is why people who are trying to break a smoking addiction will often have a sucker or gum in their mouths as temporary substitutes. Psychologists say that putting a cigarette to the lips mimics a baby's suckling. It can be very comforting. Maybe they are right.

The lady was doing well and had not smoked at all until something happened six months later that pushed her buttons. She had a really bad day. During times of stress, we sometimes turn to old coping mechanisms. We turn to a cigarette, alcohol or the half-gallon of ice cream in the back of our freezers. The lady drove to the church and caught me on a Sunday night right before I was going in to teach the youth. She said, "I have had a difficult day and I really do want a cigarette. Would you pray with me? I am desperate!"

I said, "Sure, I can pray with you, but would you mind waiting for an hour or so? I am about to go in and teach the youth. They are waiting for me."

She seemed flustered, but said, "Okay."

As I was walking into the room to teach the students, I said a quick prayer and asked the Lord to be with her until we could get together. She came back a while later just as I was cleaning up from the evening. She said, "You are never going to believe the hour that I just had. I was frustrated with you because you wouldn't pray with me when I wanted you to. I thought if I could just have one cigarette it would take the edge off and I would be all right. So I made up my mind then and there to go and buy a pack of cigarettes. I got into my car and went to Wal-Mart. I was fighting within myself, however, and thought *I don't need to go straight over to the cigarette counter. I should buy some things that I need at the house.* That's what I did. I got a buggy, picked up few things and headed straight to the cigarette counter. Guess what happened?"

I said, "I have absolutely no idea."

She said, "Well, I ran right into the couple who are my accountability partners from our Sunday school class. Can you believe it?"

I chuckled and said, "Yes, I can believe it."

She continued, "I was busted and frustrated, because now I couldn't buy cigarettes. We got in line together and checked out. I paid for my things and got into my car. I was still determined to buy a pack of cigarettes. I drove to the convenience store near my house and reached in the backseat to get my wallet. I could not find my wallet anywhere! I drove home angry and feeling sorry for myself. It was a terrible end to a very bad day."

"So, what happened?" I asked.

She said, "When I got home my husband met me at the door. He was holding my wallet in his hand. He asked, 'Did you lose something? A really nice gentleman I have never met before stopped by and dropped it off. He found it in the Wal-Mart parking lot.' It dawned on me that God had run interference for me. He blocked my way so I wouldn't fall back into that addiction. He knew it would be worse for me than it was before. I am so thankful! I just had to come and tell you."

I said, "What a great story of God's faithfulness! Thanks for telling me." We prayed together about the things that had happened during her day and she left with a sense of peace.

When things in life become difficult or stressful, it is easy to return to our old habits and ways of thinking. When our minds and emotions begin drifting in that direction it is important that we stop, take a deep breath and reassess the situation. Fear is one of the greatest tools Satan has in his arsenal. He will remind us of the awful things that might happen. He pounds our minds with disturbing thoughts and fearful images. I had a terrible time dealing with fear when I was younger until I realized that fear was not the problem. I had a love issue.

> *There is no fear in love; but perfect love casts out fear, because fear involves torment. But he who fears has not been made perfect in love. We love Him because He first loved us.*
> *—1 John 4:18-19 (emphasis mine)*

Perfect love casts out fear. What a revelation! If we are full of fear, we do not understand how much God loves us; we should think about things from God's perspective. We are God's children and He is a wonderful father. Our Father wants what is best for us. We can expect Him to nurture and take care of us. This expectation will move us forward into faith. If we dwell on the negative possibilities, we move backwards away from love and into fear. Fear will steamroll us into anxiety and sometimes even into a full-blown panic attack. How do we overcome?

First, identify the lie or the thing we fear.

Second, replace the lie with the truth.

Third, come into agreement with the truth.

I will boldly say it out loud. It reminds Satan that he is wasting his time trying to trick me. I know God loves me. I know God desires good things for me. I know Jesus died on the cross for me. I am in a covenant relationship with Him. Even if I have made poor decisions, God loves me. He is willing to forgive me if I ask Him. He will help me move my life in a direction that will be the best for me.

Once I have talked everything over with the Lord and committed it to Him, a peace will settle over me. I am encouraged through the Holy Spirit. Once I begin to celebrate and look forward to the Lord meeting my needs and answering my prayers, I get excited. It feels as though the Holy Spirit is doing cheerleading routines within my spirit. Holy Spirit excitement! I am like a kid anticipating his birthday.

"Is it my birthday yet?"

"How many more days until my birthday, Mom?"

"What's going to happen?"

I am filled with love! My prayers become charged with expectation. I no longer dwell on the negative thoughts that once consumed my mind. I now talk with the Lord and dream about His unlimited possibilities!

"So be sure when you step, Step with care and great tact. And remember that life's A Great Balancing Act. And will you succeed? Yes! You will, indeed! (98 and ¾ percent guaranteed) Kid, you'll move mountains."
—Dr. Seuss, *Oh, The Places You'll Go!*

Chapter Eighteen

GOAT TRAILS, GIN BOTTLES AND A GRIST MILL

"One of the great wonders of Christianity is that you were born into your times, to set your times aright."
—John Eldredge,
*Killing Lions: A Guide Through
the Trials Young Men Face*

God loves to answer prayer. The more desperate the need, the more impossible the situation, the bigger the dream, the more unlikely the miracle—these opportunities thrill God.

Great prayers are those that require divine intervention. Sometimes, however, if we want God to answer our prayer we must <u>do</u> something. We must take a step of faith. Some things the Lord asks us to do may scare us. Peter had to step out of the boat in order to walk on the water. Peter pushed his fear aside, took a leap of faith, and was forever changed.

A woman, who needed money so her sons would not be taken as slaves, gathered empty jars from her neighbors as Elisha had instructed. As she poured what little remained of her olive oil, God filled every empty jar. Her sons were saved (2 Kings 4.)

Peter threw a fishing line into the sea as Jesus instructed. The fish he caught had a four-drachma coin in its mouth. How bazaar is that? Peter used the money to pay the taxes (Matthew 17:24-26).

A family ran out of wine at a wedding feast. The servants filled six, twenty-gallon stone jars with water. Jesus turned the water into wine (John 2:1-12).

The priests who were traveling with Joshua needed to cross the Jordan River. The Lord said to Joshua, "Tell the priests who carry the Ark of the Covenant: 'When you reach the edge of the Jordan's waters, go and stand in the river.'" The priests did as instructed and stood in the water. The river parted and they walked across on dry ground (Joshua 3). Sometimes, if we want to see a miracle, we will need to get our feet wet.

This may sound silly, but I set aside ten dollars one time so I could go and see a movie. I had really been looking forward to it. I was on my way when I saw a dirty, skinny homeless person. The Lord spoke to me and said, "Will you give the homeless man the ten dollars you set aside?" I did, of course, and tried not to be disappointed about missing the movie. A few minutes later, a friend called me. She invited me to go and see the same movie and then took me to dinner. God blessed me with the movie and a delicious meal! Sometimes we must wade out into the water, fill a jar, go fishing, or give ten dollars away if we want to become a part of what God is doing. We must never underestimate what God will do through our acts of obedience.

Underestimating God is easy to do. This was never more apparent to me than in the first experience I had planting churches in Northern Ghana. Here are excerpts from my journal.

We left early in the morning and headed into the African bush. We were on our way to plant churches. It rained the other day, a little unusual for this time of year. It was enough to rinse the dirt off of everything and give a clean appearance. We welcomed not having the dust in our faces as we traveled.

I strapped several Bibles to the back of a motorcycle, and then climbed on to ride with Pastor Mark. We are blessed because the Bible has been translated in the language of the tribal areas where we were going. That is not true for many places.

Oswald, a pastor from Accra, rode on another motorcycle with another Ghanaian man whose name I cannot pronounce, much less spell. We had been told there was a village up a certain path and he was going to help us find it. We shooed the goats away and traveled for a long time down paths that were more trail than rutted road. We stopped at a little village along the way and bought fuel for the motorcycles. They poured it out of two old gin bottles.

When entering a village, one must get permission from the chief to assemble the people. If he does not give us permission, then we move on to another village. Once we have permission, it is a common courtesy to meet close to the chief's palace. By palace I mean a slightly larger grouping of mud huts with thatched roofs.

Both Mark and Oswald speak English and translated for me. Mark said, "There is a lot of competition between the villages. If they hear a church has been planted in a neighboring village, they want to plant one in their village. The people will tell you that if a church comes then good things will begin to happen in the village. God set this up and it works in our favor."

We arrived in the village and Mark and Oswald talked with the tribal chief, who in turn, gave us permission to meet under a large Baobab tree. Mark asked me to walk through the village and gather the people. I was the only white person in a sea of black faces, so it drew a lot of attention. I was told that most of the people in the northern tribes live in such remote areas that they have never seen a white person before. It was true. The children, full of curiosity, came up and touched my skin and pulled the hair on my head and arms. Three little boys, barefooted and wearing only shirts, kept at a distance. I took my sunglasses off, thinking it might make them feel more at ease. They all looked terrified and then turned and ran away. It didn't dawn on me until then that they had never seen blue eyes before. It must have been scary for them.

I didn't have a translator with me, so I waved at each person to say hello and motioned him or her in the direction of the tree where everyone was gathering. Many of the women were only covered from the waist down. One woman had a baby sitting on her hip and suckling her breast. Word began to spread and villagers began to come in from the fields.

As the villagers slowly made their way there, Mark and Oswald began to clap and sing Christian songs in their native language. Some of the villagers began to sing along. I asked Mark, "How they do they know the words to that song?"

He said, "They heard the song on the radio. They do not know what it means, but they liked the music so they remembered it." I noticed a small transistor radio hanging nearby on a pole barn next to the thatched roof.

The women were the last to arrive, as they took time to dress. Pastor Mark whispered, "They put on their best clothes out of respect for you." None of the clothing matched, but most of it was very colorful.

The villagers got up one by one and began dancing in a big circle. They are poor, so they do not have drums. They clapped and danced anyway, even showing us their tribal dance. One of the villagers brought some plastic chairs so I didn't have to sit in the dirt. They are very respectful and courteous, taking time to shake my hand and offering water for me to drink. It is a cloudy brown color, so I decline by showing them a bottle of water that I brought with me. I didn't want to offend them. They seemed satisfied.

Pastor Mark told the villagers, "The Lord Jesus loves you so much that he sent Misty all the way from America and Pastor Oswald from Accra and I came from Bimbila. You are on God's mind. We are Baptists who have come to tell you that we love you." We were very excited to learn that no one in the village had ever heard about Jesus.

He invited Oswald to preach. Oswald gave a simple message. He pointed to the path we had come up and said, "Just like the path that we traveled is the only way to your village, there is only one way to heaven. That way is through Jesus Christ. He is the way, the truth and the life." The moment Oswald began speaking, the presence of the Holy Spirit fell on the place. It was almost overwhelming and so wonderful! I could tell the villagers were surprised by what they were experiencing.

He spoke for about six minutes, then Mark stepped up and asked, "Would you like to ask Jesus to come into your heart and be a part of your life?" Every hand went up in the village.

Mark said, "We should never be ashamed of our commitment to the Lord Jesus, so stand up if you really mean it." They all stood. They were very excited!

Mark asked, "Would you like to meet like this again?"

They said, "Yes!"

Mark said, "Meeting together like this is called church. Would you like to have church each week in your village?"

They all said, "Yes!" They talked among themselves and decided they would meet under a mango tree on Sunday morning around ten o'clock.

Then Mark said, "We need three men to volunteer to lead the church. Can anyone here read?" One man raised his hand. Mark gave him a Bible in his own language and said, "You will need to read this Bible and teach them about it each week."

I asked Mark, "Do you invite the women to be leaders?"

He said, "No, but we can." The women are not treated very well in this country so I felt it was important to give them a voice.

He said to the villagers, "Now we would like two women who would like to lead." They were surprised and began to talk amongst themselves. They eventually pointed at two of the women and they both stepped forward. They were very reserved and cautious, keeping their eyes to the ground, but there were smiles on their faces. I can only imagine what it must have been like for them to receive validation.

Mark said, "If you promise to love and support the new leadership of the church, please raise your hand." They all agreed.

Oswald and I placed our hands on each new leader and prayed for them, "Lord Jesus, we thank you for these new leaders and ask that you will fill them now with the Holy Spirit and anoint them for the tasks that are ahead of them."

I couldn't believe it. We had planted a church in around twenty minutes! They thanked us for coming and Mark told them that he would check on them very soon and we left. A pastor was always assigned to oversee each church.

I kept thinking to myself, "The folks in America are never going to believe this. God shows up and this actually works!"

I asked Pastor Mark, "Were you saved in this way?"

He said, "Yes, some missionaries came to my village one day and did the same thing that we just did here. They planted a church that is still going strong. Planting churches is easy. I have planted ten churches in one day before. Traveling to them is what is difficult to do and takes time." Mark is a key leader in this ministry and oversees 130 churches.

We planted five churches that day; two churches in Ghana and three in the neighboring country of Togo. It is interesting that the Lord always provided one person in each village who could read. The guard we talked to at the Togo border was a Christian and let me into the country without a visa, which is required. I love the favor of the Lord.

I was still processing what I had just experienced and asked, "Mark, is it always this easy?"

He said, "Yes, because the Lord goes before us. We went to a village one time and a man and a woman were the only two people who came forward to be saved. We gave them a Bible, but had to leave because the rains were coming. We went back to check on them after the rainy season, when the roads were passable, and the church was meeting faithfully every Sunday. They had about thirty-two members. The couple told us that they had a dream the night before we came to their village. The man said, 'I dreamed that my father came to me and told me that people would be coming to the village the next day. They were going to offer me a gift and that I must take the gift. Then you came and gave me the gift of Jesus Christ.' God moves people even through their dreams."

Later, another missionary I worked with told me, "One time we got permission from the tribal chief so we could gather the people. When we got there, they were all sitting under a tree and singing, 'We know there is a Savior, won't someone come and introduce us to Him, won't someone come, won't someone come.'"

He said, "I just stood there and cried."

The pastors here in Ghana simply expect God to be God for them. They cannot do anything without Him. It has been very humbling for me. I wonder how many times I have thought to myself, *Well, that is never going to work*, or perhaps, *That is never going to happen.* How many times have I closed the door of opportunity in God's face through my disbelief?

I traveled with a group of Americans who had come over to help us at one time. I watched an entire village of people get saved as a fourteen-year-old girl read about Jesus from a Christian children's book. Sometimes we do not do things because we do not feel qualified, or gifted. It is not about our gifts, talents or education. It is about releasing ourselves to be used by the Holy Spirit and trusting Him to go ahead of us and prepare the fields for harvest! God can and will do more than we will ever ask or imagine!

I got a phone call from Dora, who is one of the ministry's area leaders here in Ghana. Dora is a person with tremendous faith. She went into the bush and established a prayer camp by building little mud huts with thatched roofs. People travel for miles, even walking the whole way, to come and stay at her prayer camp. They want to be healed.

Dora called and said to me, "Pastor, I know that I am supposed to meet with you, but I cannot come."

I said, "Okay, we can reschedule." It is a long journey and I knew it might be difficult for her to make the trip. I inquired, "Is everything okay?"

She said, "Yes. They have brought a dead woman and a demon possessed man to me and it is important that I stay here right now."

I said, "No problem. I will pray the Lord will give you wisdom so you will know what to do."

We met at a women's gathering a few weeks later and I asked, "Dora, would you mind telling me about the dead woman that they brought to you?"

She said in a very matter of fact manner, "I prayed for her and she got up."

I asked, "What happened?"

She said, "The woman was going to get water from the river and she fell over as if someone has pushed her. When they checked her she was dead. They picked her up and took her to the clinic."

The doctor examined her and said, "She is dead, go and bury her."

They said, "No, we are taking her to Dora." That is what they did.

I asked, "How long did you pray for her before she was resurrected?"

She replied, "Three hours. Her sister was there with me. She does not speak English, but would you like to meet her sister?"

I said, "Yes."

We were introduced. Dora translated for me as the woman said, "My sister was dead but now she is alive." The woman and her sister, who was raised from the dead, are both Christians.

I asked Dora, "What happened with the demon possessed man?"

Dora replied, "The man was so possessed that he would tear apart goats with his bare hands. They kept him tied up because he was always trying to strangle people."

I asked, "What did you do?"

She said, "I prayed with him and now he is free."

I asked, "How long did you have to pray with him?"

She said, "For five days."

Praying with people so they would be healed, delivered or raised from the dead were common occurrences for Dora. She had extraordinary faith! I heard story after story about wonderful things that happened at her little prayer camp. Dora is a woman of great strength.

While I was in Ghana, I put together a little team of women and we went out to the villages and spent time teaching the women. We taught them the Bible and about how they could come together and combine their money in order to help one another to learn a trade, start a business or get an education.

Many of the women had given their lives to Jesus, but many of their husbands still wanted them to go to the fetish priest and participate in the African Traditional Religion and worship the evil spirits. We encouraged them to love their husbands and trust God through it. We heard amazing personal testimonies throughout the year of what God did in marriages.

We had energetic conversations about family planning and using birth control. To some tribes, having children has become a competition. They seem to honor those women who have given birth to the most children. However, for most of the women it is their husbands who are the problem. The men in the northern part of Ghana are responsible only for the growing and providing the grain for the family, and since everything is done by hand they want children to work the fields. The women are responsible for doing literally everything else. As more and more people become Christians, this way of doing things is slowly changing.

We were with a gathering of women one time and one woman said, "I do not want to have any more children, but my husband insists that I do. If I go to the clinic to get the free birth control, my husband beats me. I do not know what to do."

Dora spoke up and said, "My husband was the same way. I had one child and then I got pregnant again. I gave birth to twins. I told my husband that I did not want to have any more children. He told me that I could not stop with twins, I had to have another child."

I leaned over to Charity, who was translating for me, and asked about this and she said, "Everyone knows that it is bad luck to stop with twins. You must have one more child."

Dora continued, "I told him I would have one more child. I got pregnant again. I had twins again! Now I had five children and I told my husband I did not want any more children."

He said, "You have to have one more child, we cannot stop with twins!" He was very determined.

Dora said, "I got pregnant again and I had twins again. [Yes, she had three sets of twins! This is something that is very rare.] So right after the birth, I told the midwife to do what she needed to do so I would not get pregnant again. I never told my husband. He died a short time later and now I am a single parent raising seven children!"

Dora told the women, "Do not let what someone else thinks keep you from doing what is right. If you do not have enough money to feed your children now, then do something about it and stop having children." Dora encouraged the women to think for themselves and not simply do what was expected.

I talked with Dora as I was preparing to move back to America. I could not imagine how difficult life was for her. Hoeing stubborn dirt and planting the fields by hand, raising seven children, and taking care of all of the people who came for prayer was exhausting. Dora did not demand money in exchange for prayer. Praying was her ministry. The people were very poor but someone might bring cassava, yams or a chicken or goat to help with food.

I said, "Dora, you have been very patient with me and I have learned so much from you. I would like to do something for you. Please pray and ask the Lord about it and then let me know what you need."

She said, "Yes, I will talk with the Lord about it and get back with you."

She called me a couple of weeks later. "I would like a grist mill."

Corn, cassava, nuts and other things were always pounded by hand using a large mortar and pestle. If she had a mill that would grind these things, she could make money to support her family and her ministry. She would not have to spend long hours doing backbreaking work in the fields.

I said, "I will ask the Lord to provide enough money to buy the equipment, run electricity to your prayer camp, pour a concrete foundation in your building, and build concrete block walls instead of mud and a zinc roof instead of thatch."

I worked out all of the details while I was there and asked my friend John to oversee the work. When I got back to America I shared this dream with people as I talked with groups about my experiences in Africa. People gave five dollars here and ten dollars there and pretty soon I was able to wire the money. The work was finished and John told me Dora is prospering today. Praise God!

The more faith we have, the more we will pray specifically. Each time our prayer is answered, God gets the glory. If our prayers are vague, we attribute everything to happenstance or coincidence and we will never grow in faith. Absolutely nothing is impossible with God. He is not limited at all in what He can and will do.

The people I met and worked with in Africa honestly believe that God is who He says He is and that He can do what He says He can do. They depend upon Him for their very survival. They need Him. Living at that place of need is a wonderful place to be, because it is the jumping off place for miracles. It is healthy to expect things from God. We should never put Him in a box and require Him to do things in a certain way. We serve an odd God. He is creative and full of wisdom. We must learn to expect the unexpected.

I was at a worship service in America one time when a man noted for a healing ministry was there to preach and pray for people. I was asked to step up on the platform and assist him. It was wonderful to see people receive healing throughout the service and to hear them talk about their experiences. At one point the pastor said, "The Lord just told me that some of you here have cavities in your teeth that need fillings. The Lord is going to fill those cavities with gold. If you have a cavity, please come forward."

With that several children came up, along with four adults. The pastor asked me and others who were helping if we would look inside their mouths for cavities. We did. One of the little boys, especially, had noticeable cavities. I wondered if he had ever seen a dentist. The pastor then looked at those who came up and simply said, "Teeth be filled in Jesus' Name." He did not look inside their mouths, but said, "Now run back to the bathroom, look inside your mouth and come back and tell me what you see." They all scurried off and came back right away with odd smiles and looks on their faces.

He asked, "Did Jesus fill your cavities with gold?"

All but one exclaimed, "Yes!"

I looked inside their mouths and sure enough there were gold fillings in their teeth. He asked the lady, "You don't have gold fillings in your teeth?"

She said, "No. As I was walking back to bathroom I told God I did not want gold in my teeth. I wanted white enamel, so that's what He gave me." The whole place erupted in laughter. God really does have a sense of humor. Can you imagine what a testimony that was for everyone at their dentists' offices? No one uses gold to fill teeth anymore. It pays to expect the unexpected and to not put God in a box.

Gold fillings? Really? It sounds ludicrous, doesn't it? It begs to ask the question: Is your limited thinking limiting God? Do you really expect anything from Him? Somewhere along the way I went from simply believing in Jesus to becoming His disciple. One scripture at a time, one step at a time, one act of obedience at a time, and over time my mind was renewed. I was no longer that small child toddling down a desolate road, trying to find my way. I had become a child of the King, running expectantly to my Abba, my heart full of love and anticipation. I am still learning, but I want to be the best disciple that I can be. Being a disciple of Jesus is not easy, but it is powerful, it is fulfilling, it is life changing!

What is the difference between being a disciple or a follower of Jesus? A disciple of Jesus will ask Him to direct her path. A believer will usually make her own decision and then ask God to bless the path that she has chosen.

Disciples live to please God, instead of living to please themselves.

Disciples make decisions out of conviction, instead of out of convenience.

Disciples do things out of obedience, rather than obligation.

Disciples honor the Word of God and do not give in to worldly opinions.

Perhaps now would be a good time for you to take stock of your life. Are you living for Jesus or are you living for yourself? Do you love Him recklessly and passionately, or are you going through the motions of an unfulfilled life? What are you praying toward? Are you making a kingdom difference? How is your faith? I pray you will take a moment and be completely transparent with Him. He knows your heart. If you do not know Jesus, perhaps this is a good time take a step of faith and entrust your life to Him. He loves you so much and has amazing things in store for you!

Helen was a disciple of Jesus. He was her "all in all." I told the Lord that I wanted to be like Elisha asking for Elijah's mantle (2 Kings 2). Perhaps He would let me wear Helen's mantle. This little lady from Birmingham, Alabama with a very large faith and an intimate relationship with Jesus set such an example that it changed my life and the lives of countless other people. It gave me a deep hunger to understand the ways of God and to be blessed enough to experience the things that Helen experienced. I wanted to live a life filled with adventure, miracles and countless answered prayers. Do you want that kind of life?

Stormy and I went to visit Helen when she was around ninety years old. She was in the hospital side of the retirement community where she lived. Although older and fragile, she still had the same warm smile and twinkle in her eyes. She reached out to us from her bed and we went over and gave her a big hug.

We talked a while and then Helen said, "There is a scrapbook over in that chest of drawers, it has a brown cover. Would you get it for me?"

"Certainly." Stormy walked over, opened the drawer and got the book.

As Helen took the book she said, "Would you mind telling me if you know who some of these people are? Would you tell me about my life?" Emotions welled up inside. How does one find the words to honor such a life? Stormy helped Helen open the scrapbook and there on the front page of the book was a photograph of Stormy and her son Jordan when he was a little boy. Tears ran down our faces. We took turns telling stories of Bible studies, vegetable soup, lamb chops, Red Lobster, greeting cards, and miracles. She would laugh and say, "Really? God did that?" It was the first time in my life that I felt I had done something for her. She was always the one changing my life and giving to me. We laughed and cried, laughed and cried, laughed and cried. We celebrated her life and praised Jesus for a long time.

A nurse passing the room noticed our tears and came rushing in, "Is everything all right?"

We reassured her, "They are happy tears."

The nurse said, "You don't understand. This is a special woman. We have to take care of her."

More tears came as Stormy and I nodded our heads in agreement, "Yes, she is."

"No, I mean she is really special." She wanted desperately for us to comprehend what she was saying. "Most people in this place are negative and complain and are just plain mean! They are awful to the people who work here, but not Ms. Helen. She is different. She is sweet and kind and joyful! I help to bathe her and do you know what she does? She prays for me. "'Lord, thank you for sending this wonderful servant of yours to help me. She has a wonderful heart and a good soul. Bless her in everything she does.'

"She blesses me the entire time I am bathing her," the nurse said. "Even during those times when she feels bad and doesn't know who she is, she still prays for me. We have to take good care of Ms. Helen, we certainly do." We all agreed and were thankful for the time that we had with her.

Helen went to be with Jesus, the love of her life, a couple of years later. I can only imagine her homecoming celebration. No presidents, kings, or famous people darkened the doorway on her deathbed. No, the hallway was filled to the brim with regular folk, custodians, nurses, handymen, students, teachers… They waited patiently to visit her one more time, and see her sweet face, to hold her wrinkled hand, desperately hoping they could find the words to tell her how she had changed their lives. Helen did not create a simple ripple in a pond. Her life created a wildfire, spreading out in every direction for generations to come. What a difference one extraordinary life of faith can make.

BOOK SUMMARY

Our journey toward faith begins when we earnestly pursue an intimate relationship with Jesus. Everything we need comes from that intimacy. As we study the word of God, our minds are renewed and we begin to see things as He sees them. We open our hearts to receive the love of Jesus and He, in turn, empowers us to love others. We learn of the covenant that He made with us and with generations before us; one in which He will never renege. We feel unconditionally loved, accepted and protected and want to please Him. We trust Him. Listening to His still, small voice, we are obedient. Our discernment grows, we recognize when our enemy Satan is prodding us toward legalism, and we take authority over his evil schemes. Confident now, we step out in faith and watch God do extraordinary things through the power of the Holy Spirit. Our expectation grows and we become more loving and generous toward others. God honors our generosity and responds by giving us the desires of our hearts. It is impossible to out give God. He is a generous and loving Father.

There is no spooky, spiritual mumbo jumbo or scientific formula for living by faith. Faith comes from knowing who Christ is and from knowing who we are in Christ. We are deeply loved by Him and every good thing in life comes out of that love.

Bibliography

Ten Boom, Corrie. *Clippings from My Notebook.* Nashville: Thomas Nelson, 1982

Meyer, Joyce. *The Wisdom of Making Right Choices – Trusting God to Led You.* (Four part cd teaching series) Fenton, Missouri, N.D.

Lucado, Max. *Traveling Light.* Nashville: Thomas Nelson, 2006

Swindoll, Charles. *Swindoll's Ultimate Book of Illustrations & Quotes – Over 1,500 Outstanding Ways to Effectively Drive Home Your Message.* Nashville: Harper Collins, 2003

Lewis, C. S. *The Magician's Nephew (The Chronicles of Narnia).* New York: Bodley Head, 1955

Manning, Brennan. *The Ragamuffin Gospel: Good News for the Bedraggled, Beat-Up, and Burnt Out.* Colorado Springs: Multnomah Books, 1990

Lucado, Max. *Grace: More Than We Deserve, Greater than We Imagine.* (Chapter Ten Chosen Children) Nashville: Thomas Nelson, 2012

Stewart, Jon: *The Daily Show with John Stewart,* Political comedy– (1996 – 2015) – Mad Cow Productions, New York City, New York, N. D.

Piper, John. *The Pleasures of God: Meditations on God's Delight in Being God.* Colorado Springs: Multnomah, 1991

Warren, John Paul. www.topfamousquotes.com. John Paul Warren Ministries. Orlando: N.D

Manning, Brennan. *All Is Grace: A Ragamuffin Memoir.* Colorado Springs: David C. Cook, 2011

Rushdie, Salma. *East, West.* New York: Random House, 1994

Fargo, Tim. *Alphabet Success Keeping it Simple, My Secrets to Success.* Published by Tim Fargo: Florida, self-published, 2014

Martin, Steve. *15 Funniest Steve Martin Quotes.* www.lists-galore. com, Sunday, July 19, 2009

Swindoll, Charles R. *Insight for Living broadcast*, Insight for Living Ministries. Plano, Texas, N.D.

Shakespeare, William. *Macbeth, Act 5, Scene 5, The Complete Works of William Shakespeare (1607 England).* Hertfordshire: Wordsworth Editions Limited, 1996

Havner, Vance (1901 – 1986) www.vancehavner.com. Ada, MI: N.D.

Spurgeon, Charles. *The Spurgeon Archive*, www.spurgeon.org, Kansas City, Missouri, N.D.

Lewis, C. S. *Mere Christianity.* New York: Harper Collins, 1952

Stanley, Andy. *It Came from Within: The Shocking Truth of What Lurks in the Heart.* Colorado Springs: Multnomah Book, 2006

Welles, Orson, (1915 – 1985), www.goodreads.com, San Francisco: N.D.

Nouwen, J. M. *The Way of the Heart: Desert Spirituality and Contemporary Ministry.* New York: HarperCollins, 1981

Snicket, Lemony. *Horseradish.* New York: HarperCollinsPublishers Children's books, 2007

Stockett, Kathryn. *The Help, A Novel.* New York: Penguin Group, 2009

Watterson, Bill. *The Complete Calvin and Hobbes.* Kansas City, Missouri: Andrews McMeel Publishing, 2005

Schulz, Charles M. Indianapolis, Indiana: Published by Saturday Evening Post, N.D.

Lewis, C.S. *The Chronicles of Narnia - The Last Battle*, New York: Harper Collins Children's Books, 1956

Twain, Mark. *Pudd'nhead Wilson.* New York: Start Publishing 2012 LLC, (1895 originally)

Omartain, Stormie. *Prayer Warrior.* Eugene, Oregon: Harvest House Publishers, 2013

Twain, Mark. From his essay *"Concerning the Jews."* New York: Harpers (now Harper Collins Publishing), 1899

Carmichael, Amy (1867 – 1951), Dohnavur Fellowship, India – Gospel Fellowship Association, www.gfamissions.org, www. goodreads.com, San Francisco: N.D.

Piper, John. *Seeing and Savoring Jesus Christ.* Wheaton, Illinois: Crossway Books a division of Good News Publishers, 2004

Reagan, Michael. *The Words of Ronald Reagan: The Wit, Wisdom, and Eternal Optimism of America's 40th President.* Nashville: Thomas Nelson, Inc., 2004

Lee, Harper. *To Kill a Mockingbird.* New York: Grand Central Publishing a division of Hatchette Book Group, 1960

Mullins, Rich (1955 – 1997) Spoken during a concert in Luftkin, Texas (July 19, 1997)

Moody, D. L. (1837 – 1899), Spoken while preaching, Chicago, Illinois, N. D.

Omartain, Stormie. *Lead Me, Holy Spirit.* Eugene, Oregon: Harvest House Publishers, 2012

Meyer, Joyce. *Battlefield of the Mind: Winning the Battle in Your Mind.* New York: Warner Books, 1995

Elliot, Elisabeth. Gateway to Joy Radio Broadcast. Bible Broadcasting Network. Charlotte, North Carolina, N.D. www.elisabethelliot.org

Elliot, Elisabeth. *Quest for Love: True Stories of Passion and Purity.* Grand Rapids, Michigan: Baker House, 1996

Swindoll, Charles R. Insight for Living broadcast, Insight for Living Ministries. Plano, Texas: N.D.

Oke, Janette. *Love Comes Softly.* Ada, MI: series, Bethany House a part of Baker Publishing Group, 1979

Wagner, Alisa Hope. Faithimagined.com, 2006
Meyer, Joyce. Enjoying Every Day Life Television Broadcast, wwwjoycemeyer.org, N.D.

Manning, Brennan. *The Ragamuffin Gospel: Good News for the Bedraggled, Beat-up, and Burnt Out.* Oregon: Multnomah Publishers, 2005

Nouwen, Henri J.M. *Bread for the Journey: A Daybook of Wisdom and Faith.* New York: HarperCollins, 1997

Eisenhower, Dwight D. www.eisenhower.archives.gov, Abilene, Kansas,
Chan, Francis. *Crazy Love: Overwhelmed by a Relentless God.* Colorado Springs: David C. Cook Publishing, 2013_

Zacharias, Ravi. www.rzim.org - Ravi Zacharias International Ministries, Just Thinking Broadcast, N.D.

Lewis, C. S. *God in the Dock: Essays on Theology and Ethics.* HarperCollins: New York, 1972

Booth, William. www.goodreads.com, San Francisco, N.D.
Snicket, Lemony. *The Lump of Coal. New York:* HarperCollins, 2008

Bucchianeri, *E.A. Brushstrokes of a Gadfly.* Carson City, Nevada: Batalha Publishers, 2011

Elliot, Elisabeth. Gateway to Joy Radio Broadcast. Bible Broadcasting Network. Charlotte, North Carolina, N.D. www.elisabethelliot.org

Angelou, Maya. www.mayaangelouquotes.org, N.D.

Follett, Ken. *World Without End.* New York: Penguin, 2007

Stanley, Andy. *Fields of Gold.* Carol Stream, Illinois: Tyndale House, 2004

Jakes, T.D. The Potters Touch Television Broadcast. www.tdjakes.org, N.D.

Tolkien, J.R.R. *The Fellowship of the Ring.* New York: Random House, 1954

Thoreau, Henry David. Economy. Boston: Walden,1854

Covey, Stephen R. *The 7 Habits of Highly Effective People: Powerful Lessons in Personal Change.* New York: Simon and Schuster, 2004

Steinbeck, John (1902 – 1968) www.goodreads.com, San Francisco: N.D.

Lewis, C.S. *Mere Christianity*. New York: HarperCollins, 1952

Twain, Mark. *The Wit and Wisdom of Mark Twain*. New York: Harper and Row, 1987

Baum, Frank L. *The Wonderful Wizard of Oz*. New York: Signet Classics published by New American Library - Penguin Group, 1900

Meyer, Joyce. Enjoying Everyday Life Broadcast, Fenton, Missouri, N.D.

Geisel, Theodor Seuss (Dr. Seuss), *Oh, The Places You'll Go!* New York: Random House, 1990

Eldridge, John. *Killing Lions: A Guide Through the Trials Young Men Face* – Unabridged Audio Book. Nashville: Thomas Nelson, 2014

CPSIA information can be obtained at www.ICGtesting.com
Printed in the USA
BVOW06s1701110116

432404BV00003B/131/P